# A Steadfast Faith

# A Steadfast Faith

The Faith Once and
for All Delivered to the Church

JUSTIN MILLER

*Foreword by Michael A. Milton*

WIPF & STOCK · Eugene, Oregon

A STEADFAST FAITH
The Faith Once and for All Delivered to the Church

Wipf & Stock
An Imprint of Wipf and Stock Publishers
199 W. 8th Ave., Suite 3
Eugene, OR 97401

www.wipfandstock.com

PAPERBACK ISBN: 978-1-4982-4122-9
HARDCOVER ISBN: 978-1-4982-4291-2
EBOOK ISBN: 978-1-4982-4292-9

Manufactured in the U.S.A.                    MARCH 21, 2019

*To my oldest son, Kaleb. As you sojourn in this world, my son,
I pray these truths capture your heart as you, by God's grace,
live a life that honors the Lord Jesus Christ in all things.*

# Contents

# Foreword

THE GREAT EXISTENTIAL QUESTIONS of life remain the most compelling. "Who am I?" "How did I get here?" "Is there a purpose to it all?" However, the most pressing question of all is "What happens when I die?" From ancient ancestors in the mountains of Europe, the expansive plains of the sub-Indian continent, the green valleys of Britannia, or the monumental deserts of Africa to the urban dwellers of Mexico City, London, and Bangkok, the question never goes away, and gets louder, it seems, with each passing generation. "What happens?" and "What must I do?" Philosophers and religious leaders have always been there, as they are with us now, seeking to provide a response. From the nihilistic voice of one like Michael Foucault, who admonishes us to "eat, drink, and be merry" for there is nothing more than what you see, to the Eastern mystics, who claim secret knowledge of the eternal and how to appease the angry gods, we are left with a veritable gumbo of answers. The problem is that the sauce in the gumbo is not hot sauce. It is poison. Yet, spiritually hungry human beings will greedily devour food laced with strychnine to fill their empty souls.

The life of Jesus of Nazareth stands out from all of this. Jesus the Christ, the Anointed One, the Messiah prophesied in the Old Testament remains the single most compelling figure in human history. Jesus claims to not only know the truth but even more: he says that *he is Truth*. Unlike other holy books, the Bible says that *Jesus is the Word* made Flesh. He lived the life we could never life—a perfect life without the least blemish—and he died the atoning death that should have been ours—atonement. But, even more, Jesus said that he would rise again from the dead on the third day. Despite, now, the well-known litany of theories about what happened to his body, the witness of history—more than five hundred people at one time—is that Jesus not only rose again from the dead, but walked the earth, ate, interacted with his friends, and continued to teach, in his resurrected state. He ascended into the clouds before the stunned band of disciples who had followed him. Each of Jesus' twelve disciples would die for the message their Master preached, except the youngest, John, who died an old man, a pastor in Ephesus.

One of the most amazing figures among those who followed Jesus, who testified to the truth of his life, death, and resurrection, was a man called Peter. Simon Peter, Bar-Jonah, was a businessman; an owner of fishing boats, to be precise. If the Bible were a fairy tale or mythology, then, the author would have made this man quite a remarkable leader. But the Bible is not a myth. The Bible is history. While claiming divine authorship, the Bible shows that God's very Word came through human beings who were not perfect, had no halos over their heads, and who often, in fact, caught up in scandalous conduct. Such was our man, Peter. Though the big Galilean brags that he will never deny Jesus, the early morning crowing of a rooster marked the Christ-predicted betrayal. Broken, laden with guilt, Peter retreats. But when the women in their small band came running back from the tomb of Joseph of Arimathea, where the Lord's body had been interred, crying out, "He has risen!" Peter races for the cemetery. He sees the empty tomb, previously guarded by Roman soldiers. With the Apostle John, Peter witnesses the winding sheets—customary burial cloths—neatly set apart. Peter believes. But Peter's story is just beginning. He would need forgiveness for the betrayal. On a beach by the familiar waters where he had so often fished before, he saw a solitary silhouette on the shoreline. The figure shouted to him to throw his net on the other side. Peter did. He and his friends pulled in such a catch that it broke the nets. And it broke the heart of the Galilean fisherman. "It is the Lord!" He dives in to swim to the shore. And there, over a humble breakfast prepared by Jesus, Peter learns what forgiveness is. Jesus shows Peter than one's love for God cannot be based on comparisons to the others. Peter's love, like yours, like mine, must be purified of ulterior motives. It was the noble Lutheran pastor-scholar-martyr, Dietrich Bonhoeffer who said that we must love God "for God's own sake." Peter is not only forgiven by Jesus through a remarkable dialogue that surely fed the mind of the rabbi, Martin Buber, who wrote about the power of "I-Thou," but he is called to shepherd the Church. From that moment, a moment not unlike the Old Testament prophet Jonah, who resisted the call of God, the Galilean fisherman becomes a pastor.

Read 1 Peter. Read that book and you will hardly recognize the author who appears in the Gospels. He is a new man. Rough-hewn before, Peter now exudes tenderness. Braggadocious before, Peter now models humility. Brash and impatient, Peter now urges the suffering saints to wait upon the Lord. Peter, who drew the sword and cut off the ear of Malchus, the Roman guard who seized Jesus, is now the one who urges believers to submit to human government and to all authorities for the sake of the Lord and the possibility to share the gospel of Jesus.

Faith in Jesus brings new life. And Peter's epistles provide the answer to the great existential questions of life. In particular, Peter shows us how to know eternal life.

I watched my mentor, Dr. D. James Kennedy, share that faith for many years. I heard that gospel from him. I have now labored to make the way of salvation and eternal life known in my own life and ministry. But what astounds me is how I am witnessing so many fine young Christian shepherds arise to carry that message to a new generation.

One of those pastors wrote the book that you are reading. The Reverend Justin Miller has prepared this book by carefully studying the writings of that man called Peter. By God's Spirit working through this young pastor, the Lord has provided us with a remarkably beautiful and concise answer to the questions "How can I be saved?" and "How can I know that I have eternal life?" Pastor Miller has followed the old fisherman whose life had been changed by the Lord of Glory, Jesus Christ, and brought back a remarkable treasure of wisdom.

I trust and pray that Pastor Miller's words will guide you to know the Way. I ask God that this study of 1 Peter 1 will help you to know the Truth. And I am certain that this book will guide those who trust in the resurrected and living Lord to know Life. For Jesus is that Word. He is that Way. He is that Truth. He is the Life that you crave.

May the Lord bless this book to the salvation of many souls so that heaven is filled with stories of redemption; stories like that of old Peter; stories like yours and mine.

MICHAEL A. MILTON, PhD
Fourth Sunday after Epiphany 2019

# Acknowledgments

JoDawn, words cannot express how grateful I am for your support and encouragement in our Lord Jesus. These books would never be possible without God's grace through you. Kaleb, Ella, Isaac, and Eden, I cannot thank God enough for you. I love being your dad and praise God for each of you. A great thank-you to Pastor Brandon for your time and labor in editing this project. Thank you, Pastor Dusty, for your help with this project. Grateful to work alongside you brothers in the kingdom of God.

# Introduction

*WHAT DOES BIBLICAL FAITH look like? How does salvation work?* I remember reading through the first Bible given to me as a young boy, trying to understand God, myself, and the world I lived in. I read from Genesis 1 through Revelation 22 and it was clear that God is "holy, holy, holy" and justly punishes sinners. I memorized the Ten Commandments and was crystal clear about being under a "holy" God's wrath. The thought of standing before God procured dread, fear, and a sense of utter hopelessness from my little heart. How could I keep my salvation after I asked Jesus into my heart? I struggled with sinful thoughts and intentions every second, every minute, and every hour in the day. Night and day I was troubled and anxious to the point I went to the pastor of the youth group where I was occasionally attending on Wednesday nights and told him about my state before God. I knew I stood condemned before God. I wanted to be saved. His response was something like this: "Invite Jesus into your life and be really sincere, and be baptized to wash away your sins." He told me that baptism was the means by which I would be saved. The day of my baptism, my first one, I will never forget coming out of the water and then walking away with the mind-set I must sin no more. The abject fear I had for God was absent for a few minutes until my mind began to dwell once more on things that were not clearly in line with the Ten Commandments. The despair, fear, and dread returned with even greater force. I wanted to cry out with all that was in me: "I cannot do this! I cannot be good enough! I cannot keep my salvation!

I cannot sin no more! Jesus is supposed to give me a great life, after all, and yet I'm still in agony on whether or not I know him!" I walked out to the car with my parents completely undone and deflated, hopeless and lost, moments after my baptism. I could not go back to get re-baptized, the church was closed now. Therefore, I eventually did what any religious person does when faced with guilt. I manufactured a system to atone for my sin before God. When I sinned, I would ask Jesus to come back into my heart and life. I had the sinner's prayer down pat. I even made sure to say it before I went to sleep, just in case. The next several years I would ask Jesus to come back into my heart every time I consciously sinned. I truly must have asked him into my heart hundreds of thousands of times. Is this really faith? Is this really how salvation works? As a young boy I thought it was and when I entered adulthood, Christianity was something I no longer took seriously or wanted anything to do with. After all, this type of God was impossible to please. He was a tyrannical deity holding my failure over me. I could not escape his wrath and judgment. I could not atone for my sin. The real problem was that I was utterly confused about how salvation worked and what biblical faith is. But by God's grace alone through his Word alone, as a young man I saw that Jesus' merit alone completely and forever makes us right with God. His work on behalf of his people procured a people for himself that endures, looking to him with a steadfast faith, which finds its source in the grace of a steadfast, glorious God. As we journey through 1 Peter 1 together, I pray your faith is strengthened as we examine what Peter conveyed to the *"aliens scattered throughout Pontus, Galatia, Cappadocia, Asia, and Bithynia, who are chosen."*[1]

1. 1 Pet 1:1.

# I

# A Steadfast Faith in a Big God and a Cross

## 1 Peter 1:1–2

> 1 *Peter, an apostle of Jesus Christ,*
>    *To those who reside as aliens, scattered throughout Pontus, Galatia, Cappadocia, Asia, and Bithynia, who are chosen*
>    *2 according to the foreknowledge of God the Father, by the sanctifying work of the Spirit, to obey Jesus Christ and be sprinkled with His blood: May grace and peace be yours in the fullest measure.*[1]

HOW DOES IT WORK!? Have you ever looked at something and asked that question? Perhaps it was a gift or a toy as a kid. You wanted to know how it worked so instead of playing with the toy you deconstructed it. You took it apart to look at all the inter-workings that made the toy do the things it did. Knowing how something works also helps us to operate it correctly. Knowing,

---

1. Unless otherwise noted, biblical passages are taken from the NASB.

biblically, how salvation works should move people to operate increasingly in line with God's will. Knowing how salvation works is vital to living rightly in light of salvation.

Today there are so many messages about "Jesus" being proclaimed. Come to Jesus and he will give you an abundant life, a life filled with healthy relationships, a great marriage, a lot of money, and a wonderful career! Ask Jesus into your heart and he will come in, forgive you of your sins, and change you! Jesus is begging to come in, just let him in! These types of message are being heralded in our Western world and exported to foreign lands. Salvation is something we decided to embrace in our own wills and is often defined as heaven later and a great life now getting what our ambitions desire and crave. It is a "Christianity" that makes man big and forgoes the cross of Christ all together. However, is a Christianity without a big God and a cross Christianity at all? A Christianity geared toward consumers fills our literature and land. Like cancer it spreads and permeates even evangelical denominations that historically have been committed to the faith. When looking at the average "church growth" methodology presented at conferences and books you will be presented with the "best" ways to garnish a crowd and grow a big church. You will be told to get a great band, have a great children's ministry, and make the messages inspiring and engaging to a person's everyday life, with the result being a big and "successful" church. The results are buildings filled with people claiming to be Christian yet devoid of any of the characteristics called for in the Holy Scripture.

Think about it . . . many make the claim, "I'm a Christian!" Millions make that claim in the Western world. According to a Gallup poll in 2017, about three-quarters of the United States claimed to be associated with Christianity, 49 percent claimed to be Protestant.[2] However, in that poll only 37 percent claimed to be dedicated to their faith. Half of Protestants classified themselves as highly religious.[3] Many people in America believe themselves to

2. Newport, "2017 Update."
3. Newport, "2017 Update."

be a Christian, yet the majority is not, if we just take Peter's depiction of what a Christian is.

I remember when it struck me that more people than I care to admit may just hear Jesus say, "I never knew you, depart from me" (Matt 7:21–23) in the region I pastor in. I was doing street evangelism and began to talk with a man who was very moral and a lifelong faithful attender of a prominent church. He told me he never missed church services and he tithed. In this moment I wanted to tell him that I have heard of such dedication before. I know of many people who are devoutly dedicated to clubs such as the rotary club, but just because you are a member there and pay your dues does not mean your ticket to heaven is punched. The man went on to describe how he had striven with all his energy to keep all the Ten Commandments his entire life. After talking with him for a little bit, I asked him the question "How do you enter heaven?" He told me, without the slightest hesitation, "Because I'm a good person who has obeyed the commandments the best I could." This man was literally heading to hell from the pews of a place of "worship." He was a member of a club called a church yet his name was not in the Lamb's Book of Life. All this may sound harsh, but it is not meant to be. The question "What is a Christian?" is important because there are millions of people who fit that scenario across our landscape today and the most unloving thing we could ever do to them is to ignore the reality of their unconverted state. There are thousands of buildings in the towns and cities called "churches" who gear all they do to attract, entertain, and keep people there feeling satisfied in their marriage, relationships, career, etc. There is so much confusion concerning what a Christian is. I heard about a testimony during a service, of sorts, in my region where a person stood up and declared how thankful they were that they were able to "stay saved" this year. The idea was that they were on their best behavior and keep the law, therefore God was pleased with them. This dilemma is not just on our side of the world either. We have transported consumer Christianity to the uttermost parts of the world.

Two years ago, as my wife and I were in Hyderabad, India, for our adoption of our youngest daughter, we had the opportunity to talk about the gospel to our guide and translator. As we talked to him about Jesus, he took out his smart phone and showed us a video of Benny Hinn and said this is Christianity. Heartbroken and discouraged, we shook our heads and said, "No, that is not Christianity at all." The definition of a Christian needs to be firmly defined. Consumer "Christianity" needs to be continuously confronted for its fraudulent claims concerning what it means to know Jesus, and the danger with regards to spreading consumeristic Christianity. The ramifications are everlasting. What worse fate than to think oneself a Christian only to face Jesus as Judge and his response to your list of accomplishments being a strong "I do not know you" followed by "Go to everlasting fire." In 1 Peter 1, Peter outlines what salvation is and how it works. He outlines what steadfast faith looks like, which is only produced by God's Spirit and God's Word permeating God's beloved people. Peter describes the operation of salvation and then calls his readers to live in light of the faith once and for all delivered to the saints.

## The Epistle of 1 Peter

Now, before we proceed into 1 Peter 1:1–2 to define what a Christian is we need to back up. Have you ever heard those debilitating words, "back up," in the middle of some profound point you were making in a conversation? Perhaps you were eloquently pointing out something profound only to find out that no one was following you as you hear those words, "back up." Before we jump into this letter to look at what a Christian is and then spend the majority of the book examining what comes forth from a Christian, we need to back up for a moment.

This great epistle was written by Simeon Peter, one of Jesus' original twelve disciples and the chief apostle, as some have called him. He wrote this letter to Christians, per v. 1, "in Pontus, Galatia, Cappadocia, Asia, and Bithynia" (1 Pet 1:1). These Christians lived in what is modern-day Turkey. Peter is most likely writing from

Rome (per the reference in 1 Pet 5:13, where Peter claims to be in Babylon) and with loving concern for what appears to be predominantly Gentile (non-Jewish) churches (1 Pet 1:18 and 4:3–4 include statements that in general would not have been made concerning Jewish background believers) going through tribulation.[4] Peter is very aware of the suffering that these Christians who were dispersed through modern Turkey were enduring (1:6–7; 2:18–20; 3:1, 13–17; 4:1–4, 12–19; 5:10).[5] Peter, filled with pastoral compassion for the flock of the Lord Jesus, wrote this letter to encourage believers to stand fast in the midst of trials and tribulations. Peter is very practical and describes how preserving faith manifests itself in Christians through "loving their neighbor"; by being good citizens, model servants, gentle wives, and caring husbands. *Peter calls these Christians to be steadfast in all areas of their life and especially in suffering.* They live out their faith in all vocations and aspects of life. Peter, in this letter, puts forth a Christianity that permeates all of a person's existence, conforming them to the image of Jesus in everything. Now that we have backed up for a moment to understand the context of this letter, let us go forward to its content and answering the question "What is a Christian?"

## What Is a Christian?

One of the greatest questions the church needs to answer is "What is a Christian?" In our genuine efforts to reach the masses we have traded biblical precision for poplar appeal, and the result has been an influx of goats into the church house, all the while the sheep are starving. Goats, whose spiritual eyes are not looking to Jesus alone for salvation and whose lives are really no different than the world around them, no matter how moral they appear to be in their own eyes, fill our pews and make decisions for our "churches." Surely on such a key issue the Bible is not unclear. The Apostle Peter answers that question in the opening verses of his epistle and then spends

4. Schreiner, *1, 2 Peter, Jude*, 20–48.

5. Schreiner, *1, 2 Peter, Jude*, 20–48.

the rest of the epistle depicting how a Christian will live in the midst of a fallen world filled with trouble and trials.

Peter states, "Peter, an apostle of Jesus Christ, to those who reside as aliens, scattered throughout Pontus, Galatia, Cappadocia, Asia, and Bithynia, who are chosen according to the foreknowledge of God the Father, by the sanctifying work of the Spirit, to obey Jesus Christ and be sprinkled with His blood: May grace and peace be yours in the fullest measure" (1 Pet 1:1–2). Peter uses some interesting phrases to describe the Christians he is writing to. He describes them as aliens who are chosen according to the foreknowledge of God the Father. This makes it clear that they are sanctified (set apart) by the work of the Holy Spirit, resulting in their obedience to Jesus Christ and being sprinkled with his blood. These characteristics describe what a Christian is, fundamentally, for all time.

## Chosen

Peter describes his audience as those "chosen according to the foreknowledge of God the Father." Remember the New Testament was penned in Koine Greek. Therefore, to really understand what Peter is saying we must return to the original language in which his letter was penned. The word "chosen" is *eklektos*, and means selected or elected. The idea is that God the Father set his heart on these people before space and time began and he did so according his "foreknowledge," which is the Greek word *prognosis*. The word foreknowledge in the original language contains the idea of "centering one's attention on."[6] Peter uses this word to describe the Father knowing the Son before the foundation of the world in v. 20.[7] God selected all those who he focused his mind on. God the Father's focus was not based on any perceived merit or decision per Romans 9:16. Before creation, God foresaw the entire human race who all were in a singular position before God, rebels deserving

6. Raymer, "1 Peter," 840.
7. Raymer, "1 Peter," 840.

A Steadfast Faith in a Big God and a Cross

judgment. God set his heart on a people as an overflow of his Triune love. God chose a people and gave his love to those people unconditionally who could never merit its worth. God set his heart on some and passed over others. Peter unequivocally presents God as completely sovereign over the salvation of his people. A theme consistent in all of Scripture. In Psalm 115:3 the psalmist says this about God: "But our God is in the heavens; He does whatever He pleases" (Ps 115:3). God rules over all the created world and he is presented in Scripture as Supreme. He is not bending his will to man's, rather he bends man's will to his. He reminded Israel of this through Moses' words in Deuteronomy 7:

> *The Lord did not set His love on you nor choose you because you were more in number than any of the peoples, for you were the fewest of all peoples,* but because the Lord loved you and kept the oath which He swore to your forefathers, the Lord brought you out by a mighty hand and redeemed you from the house of slavery, from the hand of Pharaoh king of Egypt. Know therefore that the Lord your God, He is God, the faithful God, who keeps His covenant and His lovingkindness to a thousandth generation with those who love Him and keep His commandments; but repays those who hate Him to their faces, to destroy them; He will not delay with him who hates Him, He will repay him to his face. (Deut 7:7–10, emphasis mine)

God, who is Spirit, chose Israel, as Moses reminded them, not because he saw worth in them but because he was faithful to his covenant promise and in his love toward them displayed the glory of his mercy. In essence, God told Israel he chose them to magnify what he is like to the world. God does all things for his glory and his work of salvation in Israel's existence was to draw people to himself from all nations (Exod 19:5–6; Isa 42:8). We also know that God does not change (Num 23:19). God is the one God who eternally exists as three persons and His pattern in all of redemptive history is the only True God who alone saves, changes, and ultimately brings a perfected people from all groups of people into a perfect world by his sovereign grace. (Matthew 28:19-20)

## Chosen and Adopted Is the Gospel

I mentioned earlier that my wife and I adopted our youngest girl two years ago. On that journey we were reminded over and over of God's eternal love for us. My daughter did not decide to become our child. She did not wake up one day and choose us. She didn't invite us into her heart nor did she walk an aisle making us her parents. She did nothing. She was born and cast off. Given to an orphanage where she ate one large spoon of rice a day and a couple sips of milk. She was covered with sores. To cope, she would scratch her open soars continuously as a way to soothe herself in an environment where her needs were never met. Her head was covered with lice and her belly bloated from malnutrition. She was baked in dirt. Humanly speaking, there was nothing she could offer us that would incite us toward her. At the time, she was under the category of special needs, so we assumed the future would be hard and tough. The process was long and expensive. I remember the day we picked her up at an orphanage that had conditions that were indescribably poor. I remember my wife and I looking at her and taking her into our arms. We went back to the hotel where my wife cleaned her up in the tub, treated her wounds and lice, and just held her. When she hurt, she was afraid to open her mouth because when she cried in the orphanage, they would pour hot water on her to make her be quiet. She still has those scars on her precious little body. My wife and I never quite felt the love of God like we did in those moments. We adopted my daughter and now she is disease-free, sassy, and has the biggest personality you can imagine and we adore her. Now I want to be clear. We are not some kind of hero for doing this. This is simply the gospel lived out. Every one of us who are Christians knows this story well. We were like Eden. Hopelessly in despair with wounds of our own making, covered with dirt, filled with the disease of sin. Separated from unconditional love. But God, in his kindness, adopted us to the praise of his grace through his Son. He chose us to be part of his forever family and our response to God's divine choice is that we eventually trust and love him. When Peter calls these believers "chosen according to the foreknowledge of God" this is what he has in mind. They are special because of the One who set his mind on them from eternity past.

## But, What about Missions?

I remember as a young Christian hearing about this doctrine and feeling appalled. I hated the idea of human beings having no true free will. Immediately my young mind went to, "Well wouldn't this doctrine destroy mission work around the world and evangelistic work at home?" However, in seminary and among godly brethren I was pointed to the reality that the opposite was true. Let us just look at the one person whom the Reformed movement is often labeled with. John Calvin, the pastor of Geneva during the Reformation of the church in the 1500s, is widely known for his *Institutes of the Christian Religion* and his focus on God's sovereign work in all of salvation. Unfortunately, what is not mentioned is the fact of Calvin's missional imprint from Geneva. Geneva was not a large city, nevertheless it became the missionary center in Europe during the time of Calvin's ministry, largely through religious refugees finding solace there.[8] By 1555 the population of Geneva doubled and reached a peak of around 21,000 people by 1560.[9] Calvin utilized all these religious refugees coming to Geneva to escape persecution to equip and train them for the purpose of proclaiming God's glory in salvation to the ends of the earth. In 1555, Geneva began to send ministers, trained under Calvin and approved by him, into the infant protestant movement in his beloved France. Between 1555 and 1561 much more than a hundred men were trained and sent out from the safety of Geneva to start churches in France which, at the time all of this began, had just five Reformed churches.[10] Calvin equipped these men by training them in basic Bible interpretation as well as teaching them the robust

8. Haykin, *To the Ends of the Earth*, 65.
9. Haykin, *To the Ends of the Earth*, 65.
10. Haykin, *To the Ends of the Earth*, 68.

doctrine of a gloriously sovereign God (what I'm calling a Big God in this chapter), and the cross of Christ to procure for God's glory a people for his name from all people groups. The result was by 1562 the number of Reformed churches was over two thousand and the total number of members estimated within these churches was two million, roughly 10 percent of France's population![11] Calvin, in his lectures, would have up to a thousand men attending and many of these men would go into a hostile country where their lives would be at risk of torture, imprisonment, and execution. Often services had to be conducted in homes behind locked doors. These men went into such an environment and endured because of Calvin's Big God theology that orbited the cross of Christ procuring a people for himself. The God of Holy Scripture which Calvin clearly depicted moved these men to risk it all to see people hear this good news. France was not the only location either. Calvin also sent two missionaries to Brazil, and in his writings clearly upheld the importance of the gospel going to the ends of the earth. Needless to say, the doctrine of predestination fueled, rather than hindered, the mission work in Calvin's Geneva.

I know some people may think, "Well that was just that one example, and it was a fluke." That is not the case. Since that point, many of the men that God has used in mission movements, including the father of modern missions, William Carey, all held to Calvin's understanding of God's sovereignty in salvation. The reason this doctrine fuels the fires of missionary work is that it captures men and women with the scriptural vision of a God who is supreme over all things and he has procured for himself a people won by his Son's sinless sacrifice. As born-again Christians behold these truths, there are no lengths that we will not go and there are no sacrifices that we are unwilling to pay in light of the glory of such a King, who is more beautiful than anything in this world. Therefore, we go with love and boldness to claim, by his gospel, the reward of the Son's sufferings! Adoniram Judson, William Carey, Jonathan Edwards, George Whitefield, David Brainerd, Charles Spurgeon, Martin Loyd-Jones, D. James Kennedy, John Piper, John

11. Haykin, *To the Ends of the Earth*, 69.

MacArthur, and many others, are all just a small sample of some of the most evangelistic and missional men in modern history and all held and/or hold unwaveringly to a God who is sovereign over all salvation. From Paul to Piper the great men who have poured their lives out for God's glory among all people groups knew well the God that Calvin conveyed rightly from Holy Scripture.

The truth of God's sovereign work in salvation is an inescapable truth in Scripture (Romans 9, Ephesians 1, all of the Old Testament, etc.) and it fuels the mission work of the church. Paul states in Ephesians 1:5–6 the following terms: "*He predestined us to adoption* as sons through Jesus Christ to Himself, according to the kind intention of His will, to the praise of the glory of His grace, which He freely bestowed on us in the Beloved" (Eph 1:5–6, emphasis mine). God's people are God's people because he came to us, not us first coming to him. This fuels mission work, and for believers who rest in this reality, deepens our awe of God as we see that he has chosen us to be part of his forever family. Remember in Ephesians 1:5 the end of predestination per Paul. He conveyed that we are chosen to be adopted into God's family through Jesus per the kind intention of God's will to the praise of his glorious grace. God's choosing of us is to the praise of his grace, which results in our being brought into his forever family through Jesus. We are chosen and thereby adopted by God through the cross of Christ Jesus.

## My Sheep Will Come to Me

If are you reading this and profess to follow Jesus. Think with me for a moment on the implications of this doctrine. God set his mind on you and loved you before he created the cosmos. God before time knew your name, loved you eternally in Jesus, and determined to bring you to him though there was nothing inherently worthy in you, me, or anyone. Jesus taught the amazing love of God the Father who gave those he set his heart on to the Good Shepherd Jesus in John 10:27–30, "My sheep hear My voice, and I know them, and they follow Me; and I give eternal life to them, and they will never perish; and no one will snatch them out of My hand. My Father, who has given *them* to Me, is greater than all; and no one is able to snatch *them* out of the Father's hand" (John 10:27–30). Jesus is the Good Shepherd. The people of God, his sheep, are those whom the Father loved eternally and gave to Jesus to bring into the fold of his kingdom forever. The people of God hear Jesus voice (the Word) and follow him. We as the people of God are loved eternally and unconditionally by a good Father who set his heart on us before time, not because of anything good in us (Rom 9:16), but because of his goodness and love. He set his heart on us to give us to his Son by the work of God the Holy Spirit.

## Set Apart by the Spirit unto the Lord Jesus

Peter in 1 Peter 1:2 describes the audience he is writing to as those chosen by God, "by the sanctifying work of the Spirit." The word "sanctifying" is *hagiasmos*, and means to set apart, to consecrate.[12] The Holy Spirit had set these people that Peter has penned this letter to apart. They were once part of one thing and now are part of another. The Spirit moved them from one category of people to another category of people.

### Moving Categories

Have you ever changed categories before? Moving from vary different categories such as from a meat eater to a vegetarian. Or perhaps something in our time that would be even more drastic like going from a liberal Democrat and moving over into the category of a conservative Republican. A complete shift happens in a person's thinking and life when they move from the category of meat eater to vegetarian or Democrat to Republican. In Ephesians 2:1–5, we see a before-picture of a group of people in Ephesus who began life in one category and were going to end their lives in another category that was opposite in every way of true importance.

12. Kittel et al., *Theological Dictionary*, 17.

In Ephesians 2:1–3 Paul describes these Ephesians he is writing to as dead in transgressions and sin. He conveys that they previously followed the ways of the world, gratifying their own flesh, and like the rest of humankind, were by nature children of wrath. Then comes v. 4, opening powerfully, "*But God* being rich in mercy, because of the great love with which he loved us, even when we were dead in our trespasses, made us [the church] alive together with Christ—by grace you have been saved." The Ephesians, like those Peter is writing to in 1 Peter, were once dead in sins, part of the fallen world, and under God's wrath. But God made them spiritually alive by the Holy Spirit who applied the work of Christ on the cross to them.

## Set Apart to Trust in Jesus' Finished Work on the Cross

The work of the Holy Spirit is to set apart. What exactly has the Holy Spirit set these people apart to? Peter, in the rest of v. 2, answers that. The Holy Spirit sets the church apart, "to obey Jesus Christ and be sprinkled with His blood" (1 Pet 1:1–2). Tom Schreiner describes the "setting apart" work of the Holy Spirit unto Jesus in the following way: "As the gospel is proclaimed, the Spirit sanctifies some by bringing them to faith, by bringing them into the realm of the holy."[13] Schreiner goes on to describe what Peter means by the Holy Spirit producing obedience to Jesus and sprinkling them with his blood: "Conversion is not merely an intellectual acceptance of the gospel, nor is it faith with a blank slate. Believers enter the covenant by obeying the gospel and through the sprinkled blood of Christ, that is, his cleansing sacrifice."[14] The Holy Spirit produces obedience to the gospel (faith in the finished work of Jesus) and our sin being removed before God through Jesus' atoning sacrifice (justification).

13. Schreiner, *1, 2 Peter, Jude*, 54.
14. Schreiner, *1, 2 Peter, Jude*, 56.

## *The Atonement of Christ from Isaiah 53*

When Peter conveys that these Christians were set apart to be sprinkled by the blood of Jesus, he has in mind a sacrifice made in their place to remove their guilt and sin before God for all time. The best place in all of Scripture to see what Christ Jesus accomplished on our behalf is Isaiah 53. We are particularly going to examine vv. 4–12.

> Surely our griefs He Himself bore,
> And our sorrows He carried;
> Yet we ourselves esteemed Him stricken,
> Smitten of God, and afflicted.
> But He was pierced through for our transgressions,
> He was crushed for our iniquities;
> The chastening for our well-being *fell* upon Him,
> And by His scourging we are healed.
> All of us like sheep have gone astray,
> Each of us has turned to his own way;
> But the Lord has caused the iniquity of us all
> To fall on Him.
> He was oppressed and He was afflicted,
> Yet He did not open His mouth;
> Like a lamb that is led to slaughter,
> And like a sheep that is silent before its shearers,
> So He did not open His mouth.
> By oppression and judgment He was taken away;
> And as for His generation, who considered
> That He was cut off out of the land of the living
> For the transgression of my people, to whom the stroke *was due?*
> His grave was assigned with wicked men,
> Yet He was with a rich man in His death,
> Because He had done no violence,
> Nor was there any deceit in His mouth.
> But the Lord was pleased

To crush Him, putting *Him* to grief;
If He would render Himself *as* a guilt offering,
He will see *His* offspring,
He will prolong *His* days,
And the good pleasure of the Lord will prosper in His hand.
As a result of the anguish of His soul,
He will see *it and* be satisfied;
By His knowledge the Righteous One,
My Servant, will justify the many,
As He will bear their iniquities.
Therefore, I will allot Him a portion with the great,
And He will divide the booty with the strong;
Because He poured out Himself to death,
And was numbered with the transgressors;
Yet He Himself bore the sin of many,
And interceded for the transgressors. (Isa 53:4–12)

Isaiah depicted the suffering servant as being smitten by God, pierced for our law breaking, crushed for our sins, with the judgment that is due to us falling on him (Isa 43:4–5). We, the sheep who are gone astray, are brought to our God through the Suffering Servant's sacrifice. Isaiah then shows us who ultimately was the One who crushed Jesus on the cross. In Isaiah 43:10, God the Father was pleased to crush him, for Jesus is our guilt offering. Isaiah follows that up by saying Jesus will see the offspring (a people from every tribe, tongue, and nation) come forth and he will prolong his days, which alluded to his resurrection that validated his sacrifice on behalf of his people as acceptable to God the Father. The Lord Jesus, fully God and sinless man (John 1:1, 14), who knew no sin, became sin so we may become the righteousness of God (2 Cor 5:21). Jesus, as depicted here by Isaiah, took all the sin and guilt of his people and forever satisfied God's judgment and eternal wrath in the stead of his people (Rom 3:25). God the Father then raised him back to life, communicating that he had accepted Jesus' sacrifice on our behalf and Jesus is indeed God the Son (Rom 1:4). God transfers Jesus' earned righteousness, which is his perfect obedience both active and passive under law, to his people's account upon them being set apart by the Holy Spirit through faith in Jesus. The result is seen by the Apostle John as he gazes at a people in white and hears who they are in Revelation 7:14b: "They have washed their robes and made them white in the blood of the Lamb" (Rev 7:14b). This message is truly good news. God the Son was crushed and endured the eternal judgment of God so all who are set apart to trust in Jesus will have life everlasting with God forever. Jesus died on the cross and took God's frown so we may have God's everlasting smile. That is the gospel we are set apart to. Jesus' blood was shed as our sacrifice in our place to atone for our sin. He died in his flesh in perfect obedience to the will of God and endured in his deity the eternal wrath of God, so that we may someday live in the flesh and spirit as a perfected people. The gospel is truly glorious news!

### *What Actually Is Response Called Forth in the Gospel?*
### *—Obedience to the Faith*

How do we react to such good news? How do we receive it? Peter said God's beloved were set apart "to obey Jesus Christ" in v. 2. Paul called this the "obedience of faith" in Romans 1:5 and 16:26. We know that God must work in us to respond from what Peter has said thus far, but what does obedience to Jesus mean exactly. The best place to discern what that statement means is to go to Jesus himself to see what he meant by that sort of terminology. Jesus, in John 6, is interacting back and forth with a large crowd that hunted him down because the day before he had fed thousands of bellies with a couple of loaves of bread and a few fish. They want to make him king and have him take care of them materially the rest of their days. Jesus refuses, sends his disciples across the shore, and goes up the mountain, later to walk on water to his disciples. In John 6, on the other side of the shore, the crowds look for Jesus and then cross the sea to the other side to find him. When they do, Jesus chastises them for seeking him out just to have their bellies filled. Jesus then proclaims to this large crowd, "Do not work for the food which perishes, but for the food which endures to eternal life, which the Son of Man will give you, for on Him the Father, God, has set His seal" (John 6:27). The crowd responds to Jesus and asks what works, what obedient acts do they need to do in order to receive this. Jesus, in v. 29, responds, "This is the work of God, *that you believe in Him whom He has sent*" (John 6:29, emphasis mine). Believing the gospel is not optional. It is a command of God. The gospel is a command and the only way it is obeyed is by doing what the command says. God commands everyone to believe on Jesus. The obedience of faith, as Paul called it, or as Peter said, "to obey Jesus Christ," is simply responding to the gospel by trusting in the person and work of the Lord Jesus to make us right with our Creator. The Holy Spirit is the One who gives faith to those whom God has chosen according to his foreknowledge per 1 Peter 1:1–2. This faith is a gift of God and is the channel by which God's grace flows to us, and our sin flows to his Son.

## *An Example of the Holy Spirit Giving Faith and Applying the Cleansing Work of Christ's Sacrifice*

Paul, in Acts 13, preaches in Pisidian Antioch to the Jews who consider what he says about Jesus and then go onto reject it when they see the crowds coming to hear Paul speak at the next synagogue. Paul calls out for the non-Jews to embrace the gospel. Luke, the author of Acts, recounts what happens next in precise and clear language. In Acts 13:48 Luke states, "When the Gentiles heard this, they began rejoicing and glorifying the word of the Lord; and as many as had been appointed to eternal life believed." It is easy to focus on the "they believed" part and forgot that they only believed because they "*had been appointed to eternal life*." They had been set apart by God to receive eternal life and therefore they were given faith as they heard Paul preach the gospel. It may have initially seemed to them, as it does to many of us today, to be their own willful decision and response, but in reality if we are truly spiritually dead (Eph 2:1) the only way we will respond to the gospel is for God's Spirit to make us alive and to then willfully trust in

Jesus. God's Spirit must resurrect us spiritually to produce in us a response of faith in the finished work of the Lord Jesus on the cross. The work of salvation is all the work of a Triune God.

## The Holy Spirit Takes Our Heart of Stone and Give Us a Heart of Flesh

I need more explanation! As a pastor I love when people say that. It means they want a deeper dive into what was just taught or said. It means they are not content with their current understanding and want to know more. They do not just want to take my word for it but want to see how what was just said came from Scripture rightly interpreted. We need more of an explanation on how the Spirit brings forth faith in Jesus from a person. Ezekiel 36:26–27, written hundreds of years before Jesus was born, outlines it precisely. Ezekiel 36:26–27 states, "Moreover, I will give you a new heart and put a new spirit within you; and I will remove the heart of stone from your flesh and give you a heart of flesh. I will put My Spirit within you and cause you to walk in My statutes, and you will be careful to observe My ordinances." Ezekiel describes the new covenant that the Messiah would bring whereby the Holy Spirit would give God's people "a heart of flesh," the Holy Spirit would be put in God's people, and the Holy Spirit would cause God's people to walk in his statutes and truth. In the Scripture the word "heart" is the center of the physical, mental, and spiritual life of humans.[15] The ancient Near Eastern mentality saw the heart as the seat of one's will, intellect, and affections. Therefore, in the new covenant per Ezekiel, God gives his people a new mind (way of thinking), a new will, and a new set of affections. God changes us and makes us new inwardly and this change brought by the Holy Spirit as the gospel is shared or preached causes God's chosen to respond in faith. This change produces the "obedience to Jesus Christ" which results in their being "sprinkled by His blood."

---

15. *Holman Illustrated Bible Dictionary*, s.v. "Heart" (entry by Gerald P. Cowen).

# How Do I Know If I Have Been
# Sanctified by the Holy Spirit?

At this point it is beneficial to just take a moment and ask the question "Has this happened to me?" Have I been set apart by the Holy Spirit to believe in Jesus and be cleansed by his cross of all my sin before God? I recently talked with a person on the phone who was struggling with whether or not they were saved. This individual said I do not know when God opened my heart to trust in Jesus. They struggled, like many do, with the question "Am I saved?" How do you, the readers of this book, know you are alive? Well, you are breathing! How do we know we have been born again? Today, at this moment we love Jesus with our affections (though imperfectly), we trust Jesus with our wills, and our minds are set on knowing him and growing in him. In essence we are breathing spiritually. We are clinging to Jesus and nothing else to save us from God's wrath and this is great evidence that we are breathing spiritually and have been born of the Holy Spirit. Being born again will also produce new behaviors that will follow our new affections, will, and mind. The book of 1 John was written so that the original audience, and us today, would know we are saved (1 John 5:13). He describes the born-again life as a life that loves Jesus, trusts Jesus, gets the gospel and Jesus right, and loves the church and has a growing hatred of sin (all of 1 John).

# A Christian Is an Alien

Watch any movie that centers around the idea of aliens and it usually describes a species that comes from the stars that invades the world with the aim of taking it over. I remember as a young kid watching *Independence Day* and being freaked out by the creepy alien that emerged from the ship that Will Smith's character shot down. I remember feeling disdain, as I was caught up in the movie, for the creatures that invaded the earth and cheering for the forces that fought them in order to keep mankind from extinction. We as human beings, in our imagination, come forth with these types of movies and stories, and in the human mind, are inherently tense or even hostile toward anything different from us. We are uncomfortable with those who are different from us, who see things differently, and who act differently. Just look at the social patterns of teenagers. They gravitate toward people who have the same interests as them. When I was in high school, generally the basketball players hung out together, the more intellectual kids hung out together, and the band kids hung out together. Sure there were the crossings of groups, but the existence of the groups proves the point. We by nature gravitate toward those who are like us. The church gravitates toward one another because we share the most important thing in common: faith in Jesus. The world centers around various ideologies and systems of thought, but genuine Christians are alien and invasive to the fallen world.

Per the Apostle Peter, a Christian is chosen by God. A Christian is set apart by the Holy Spirit through the gospel of Jesus unto faith and forgiveness. Per Peter, a Christian is also an "alien." Peter states, "*To those who reside as aliens*" (1 Pet 1:1–2). Peter addresses those in modern-day Turkey who reside as aliens. The word "aliens" is the Greek word *parepidēmos* and it means a person or persons who are a stranger in a foreign land.[16] This word conveys that God's people are pilgrims, sojourners, and exiles in this world we currently live in.[17] A Christian is someone who is in the world, but this world is not truly their home. We are passing through this world but do not heed its values, beliefs, and philosophies. We are altogether a peculiar people who look to and long for a time yet to come all the while faithfully living for our King in the midst of the fallen world, we find ourselves in.

Recently, at the time this was written, a missionary was killed on a remote island off India among a remote people. He went there to share the gospel per the Great Commission. The press responded to his death with sympathy, but to some degree confusion, and even anger. His death was portrayed as foolishness and meaningless. His values and commitment to share the gospel as

16. Louw, *Greek-English Lexicon*, 132.

17. Schreiner, *1, 2 Peter, Jude*, 50.

too invasive. In short, he was an alien in this world and was portrayed as such by the news media. Jesus said to his disciples in John 15:18–19, "If the world hates you, you know that it has hated Me before it hated you. If you were of the world, the world would love its own; but because you are not of the world, but I chose you out of the world, because of this the world hates you." The reality is if you are a Christian you will be odd to the world just as Jesus was odd to the world. You will be different and the world will respond in kind.

## Our Lives Should Be Alien to the World Around Us

The Christian lives a life in submission to the cross of Jesus. One of the greatest stories that is alien to the world is the story of Jim Elliot. Jim Elliot showed much promise. He was born into a great family in Portland, Oregon. Graduated in 1949 from Wheaton College. He was intellectually gifted and a great public speaker as well as a gifted writer, and a wrestling champion in college. In 1952 Jim went to Ecuador to establish a school and a Bible teaching ministry among the Quechua Indians. He married Elisabeth Howard in 1953, whose writing has given us a lot of information on Jim's thought and life in light of the cross of Christ. Jim and four companions began efforts shortly after to reach the Aucas tribe, an indigenous tribe in eastern Ecuador. After three months of weekly visits by air over the village, they landed on the beach only to be attacked and killed two days later. They refused to fight back though they had the resources to do so. Their deaths led to the conversions of several of the Aucas tribe as they saw these men willingly die to give them the gospel of Jesus. Jim's famous saying is "He is no fool who gives what he cannot keep to gain what he cannot lose."[18] To the world, Jim's passion for the spread of the gospel and his early death at twenty-eight seemed unnecessary and foolish. A wasted life with so much potential. Everything about Jim Elliot seems foreign to the world who does not know Jesus. However, to the

18. Howard, "Elliot, Philip James," 230.

Christian it was a life lived in the shadow of the Almighty. A life that carried the cross so that others may see the glory of the Savior who died on the cross. A life chosen by God, set apart by the Spirit, and redeemed by Jesus will be alien to the world and will highlight God as infinitely more valuable than anything this world has in it.

While we may not be called to the Aucas Indians we are called to live as aliens in this world. We are called to be different than the world in thought and action. The world should look at how we handle our families, our money, our time, and our lives as if we are alien. In Jim Elliot's diary he wrote the following entry, "God, I pray Thee, light these idle sticks of my life, that I may burn for Thee. Consume my life, my God, for it is Thine. I seek not a long life, but a full one, like You, Lord Jesus."[19] Is our passion for God's glory evident by how we live? Are we alien to the world, much like Jim Elliot was and the Christians Peter was writing to were?

## What Is a Christian?

The cross-less consumer Christianity is killing people's souls, literally! What a Christian needs is to be clearly defined. A Christian is eternally loved by God, set apart by God's Spirit, redeemed by the work of Christ apprehended through faith. The result will be a Christian and Christianity that is utterly foreign and fearful to the world now, but will fill the world to come with praise of the Triune God. *Christians are a cross-carrying, chosen people. We are people procured by God and kept through "a steadfast faith." Is there any better title by which we should desire to be known?*

---

19. Tan, *Encyclopedia of 7,700 Illustrations*, 271.

## Discussion Questions

1. Why is a cross-less, consumer-driven "Christianity" a fraud and dangerous?

2. What is Peter's definition in vv. 1–2 of a Christian?

3. Why does Peter refer to these Christians in Asia as aliens?

4. A steadfast faith is brought about how (how is a person "saved")?

# 2

# A Steadfast Faith in Trials with Heaven in View

## 1 Peter 1:3–9

3 *Blessed be the God and Father of our Lord Jesus Christ, who according to His great mercy has caused us to be born again to a living hope through the resurrection of Jesus Christ from the dead,*

4 *to obtain an inheritance which is imperishable and undefiled and will not fade away, reserved in heaven for you,*

5 *who are protected by the power of God through faith for a salvation ready to be revealed in the last time.*

6 *In this you greatly rejoice, even though now for a little while, if necessary, you have been distressed by various trials,*

7 *so that the proof of your faith, being more precious than gold which is perishable, even though tested by fire, may be found to result in praise and glory and honor at the revelation of Jesus Christ;*

8 *and though you have not seen Him, you love Him, and though you do not see Him now, but believe in Him, you greatly rejoice with joy inexpressible and full of glory,*

*9 obtaining as the outcome of your faith the salvation of your souls.*

HE IS TOO HEAVENLY minded to be any earthly good! Maybe that saying is not as familiar as this one: "Their head is in the clouds." The idea being conveyed here is that when we set our minds on another world (real or otherwise), we become no good to anyone in the world we live in. While it is easy to understand what may be implied, this statement concerning being distracted is entirely foreign to the Apostle Peter. Peter, in 1 Peter 1:3–9, says the exact opposite. He implies that the only way to be of any earthly good is to be completely heavenly minded. To set our focus on the kingdom to come and its King. This heavenly minded mind-set is not something that is inherently natural in human beings apart from God's gracious work in their lives. To enjoy God and focus on his kingdom we have to be "born again" as seen in vv. 1–2 of 1 Peter 1 (sanctified by the Spirit). Peter, seemingly stressing the sovereign nature of salvation, repeats the ideology he puts forth in vv. 1–2 in the opening statements of v. 3. Peter states in v. 3, "Blessed be the God and Father of our Lord Jesus Christ, who according to His great mercy has caused us to be born again to a living hope through the resurrection of Jesus Christ from the dead." Peter, in his opening statement of praise beginning with the word "blessed," outlines how God brings people to him through the process of "caused us to be born again." The new birth that Peter is talking about is the work of the Holy Spirit (John 3:3–10) to create a new heart (mind, affections, and will) in God's people foreknown from before time (Ezek 36:26–27). The Holy Spirit giving us a mind, a set of affections, and will set on God's glory in Jesus ultimately, per Peter, gives us a living hope through the resurrection of Jesus from the dead. This is all God's mercy which eliminates man's boast. Peter could not be clearer, for the phrase "caused to be born again" is in the active voice in the original language. God is the one doing this work, not man. A Christian is not someone who decided to follow Jesus in their strength or power of will, rather someone

God has chosen and, in his mercy, given them a mind, will, and set of affections that are now upon the person and work of Jesus. The hope that these believers are saved to is that, just as Jesus was raised materially never to die materially again, so shall all God's people. Our hope is Jesus himself and therefore truly a living hope, indeed! A person who is born again is one who looks to Jesus in faith and loves Jesus in adoration. Therefore, they will find their highest satisfaction not in their favorite hobbies or sports teams (not bad things necessarily in themselves) but in their relationship with Jesus. They will look to Jesus and set their gaze on him and his coming kingdom.

## What Makes Me Happy?

Have you ever intrinsically pondered, "What makes me happy?" "What do I enjoy the most in everyday life and life in general?" Let us not give the Sunday school answer here but be honest with ourselves. What do we enjoy? What do we look forward to? What do we find our identity in? Maybe your mind goes to a hobby. Maybe it is a relationship you have with a spouse. Or perhaps it is a sports team you love to watch and root for. Prayerfully, it is not the St. Louis Cardinals (as a Braves fan only the Cubs are more appalling). I know people who organize their entire calendar around their favorite baseball team's schedule. People will plan their week around their hobbies, such as fishing, hunting, golfing, etc. People will schedule vacations to get away from something, usually to go and enjoy something else. Others find their solace in their spouses and kids. Are all these things bad? No, unless they are what our highest delight and greatest joy are in. David in Psalm 37:4 states, "Delight yourself in the Lord; And He will give you the desires of your heart." God does all things for his glory per Isaiah 48:9–11 and he delights in bringing a people to see his glory and respond by delighting in him to the uttermost. The redeemed of the Lord Jesus are redeemed to the end that we will delight with the utmost joy and pleasure in the glory of God. The lens we began to view our lives is in light of everything being about the magnification of who

God is and his everlasting attributes. Paul states in 1 Corinthians 10:31 that we are to do all things for God's glory. The real-life question we need to put forth is: How do we enjoy God in the midst of our greatest trials and tragedies when we can barely lift our head up in the midst of over sorrow and suffering? Peter is writing to Christians in Pontus, Galatia, Cappadocia, Asia, and Bithynia who are entering into a season of great tribulation and suffering. He outlines to them the importance of enjoying God in light of eternity. He calls them to set their gaze on God's coming deliverance and someday consummated kingdom. Glorifying God and enjoying God are inseparably tied to one another. C. S. Lewis observes, "Fully to enjoy is to glorify. In commanding us to glorify Him, God is inviting us to enjoy Him."[1] How do we do that when we are overcome with grief in the present? Peter, in vv. 3–9, communicates to the suffering people of God in Asia to look unto the future where the kingdom of God will be fully and eternally realized.

Peter partially begins this exhortation in v. 3 as he highlights the reality that the Lord rose from the dead to never die, which implies strongly that we, who are born again, will someday be raised from the dead to a living hope void of pain and suffering in God's presence on a new earth (1 Cor 15; Rev 21–22). Peter described us as being born again to a living hope through the resurrection of Jesus from the dead. In vv. 4 and 5, he presents this hope to his readers, which is "to obtain an inheritance which is imperishable and undefiled and will not fade away, reserved in heaven for you, who are protected by the power of God through faith for a salvation ready to be revealed in the last time" (1 Pet 1:4–5). He outlines the living hope that Jesus' resurrection preceded and provides for his people, which is a new heaven and earth!

---

1. Lewis, *Reflections on the Psalms*, 86–87.

## The New Heavens and Earth Described in Three Adjectives

Adjectives are important. They give descriptions of people, places, and things. Sometimes they give descriptions of people, places, or things that are not very positive. Sometimes they positively describe something. For example, my wife is beautiful, compassionate, and kind. Those adjectives are so true of my bride that on more than one occasion I have been asked how I (a nerdy pastor) was able to woo her (a beautiful daughter of the Highest King). Just in case you are wondering, the answer is simple. God is kind to the unworthy. In v. 4, Peter outlines what is coming for believers in Jesus (glorification), which he calls an inheritance. The noun "inheritance" Peter described with the three adjectives and one participle: imperishable, undefiled, will not fade away, and reserved. Imperishable in the original language means "lasting forever" and "unable to be corrupted."[2] Undefiled is translated from the Greek word *amiantos* and it means "not morally tainted."[3] "Will not fade away" is translated from the one Greek word *amarantos* which means "will never lose its character or brightness."[4] The participle "reserved" in the original is in the perfect tense which means the inheritance we will receive in Jesus is from eternity past and has been kept in heaven for God's people with the future result of it coming down to a perfected earth! This inheritance that Peter is describing will last forever in contrast to the current world which will be destroyed by fire. The world to come will have no sin or taint of rebellion against God. No sickness or sorrow. No funerals and grave plots. It's brightness and resources will never grow dim or need to be replenished. It has been reserved by God for us and will come at the return of the Lord Jesus. What Peter describes here, John outlines in great detail in Revelation 21, as well as Revelation 22. John states:

2. Swanson, *Dictionary of Biblical Languages*, s.v. "aphthartos."

3. Swanson, *Dictionary of Biblical Languages*, s.v. "amiantos."

4. Louw, *Greek-English Lexicon*, 695.

> Then I saw a new heaven and a new earth; for the first
> heaven and the first earth passed away, and there is no
> longer any sea. And I saw the holy city, new Jerusalem,
> coming down out of heaven from God, made ready as
> a bride adorned for her husband. And I heard a loud
> voice from the throne, saying, "Behold, the tabernacle of
> God is among men, and He will dwell among them, and
> they shall be His people, and God Himself will be among
> them, and He will wipe away every tear from their eyes;
> and there will no longer be any death; there will no lon-
> ger be any mourning, or crying, or pain; the first things
> have passed away." (Rev 21:1–4)

John describes, in detail, in the first four verses of Revelation 21
what Peter called our "inheritance," which is "reserved in heaven."
That inheritance in Revelation 21:2 in line with Peter's description
in 1 Peter 1:4 comes down from its place with God to the new earth
where the Triune God will dwell forever with his perfected people
in a perfect and pure place. The terminology used here speaks of
the absolute certainty and also security of our inheritance that
Christ won for his people. As Dr. Schreiner puts it, "His point was
that they are sojourners and aliens in this world, they face suffering now, and their hope is directed to the future inheritance.
This inheritance 'can never perish' (*aphtharton*) or be corrupted."[5]
Schreiner in his commentary on 1 Peter goes on to say, "Peter
emphasized in the strongest possible terms the security and certainty of the reward awaiting believers."[6] Our inheritance is secure.
Remember, as believers die, our spirits are perfected and thereby
ushered immediately into the presence of Christ (2 Cor 5:8), but
as Peter points out, that is not our final place. Our final resting
place is not sitting on the clouds playing harps, rather it is bodily
resurrection, soul perfection, and living in an imperishable, pure
place. A place where the river of life flows from the throne of God
and the Lamb and the tree of life is once again given to man (Rev
22:1–2). A place where there is no death, no curse, and no night
(Rev 22:3–4). A place where Jesus will light up the world with his

5. Schreiner, *1, 2 Peter, Jude*, 63.

6. Schreiner, *1, 2 Peter, Jude*, 63.

glory (Rev 22:5). How does this make you feel as you read it? Do you long for such a place?

## A Deacon's Living Hope

A couple of weeks ago, I had a home visit with a deacon and his wife from the church in which I'm blessed to pastor. This deacon has faithfully served the Lord Jesus and poured out his life for the spiritual good of his brethren and, for the glory of Jesus, the community he lives in. He has faithfully served Christ and his church with the motive of being faithful. While at this home visit, he and his wife told me the news that they had recently been given. He has stage 4 cancer. As they worked through their emotions in light of such news, this faithful deacon's mind singularly kept going back to two things. First, his sole hope was in nothing else but Christ's work alone to make him right before God. He repeated it over and over again. In Jesus alone, by grace alone, through faith alone, revealed by Scripture alone to the glory of God alone. Much like a broken record that repeats a line, his heart language repeated the glorious truth of the five *solas* of the Reformation. Jesus and his work on the cross was this brother's only boast, greatest hope, and singular delight of his heart. Nothing else but Jesus. The second item he held onto was the reality that he would enter into Christ's presence with the ultimate end that he would live in Christ's perfected world as a perfected person. It is our hope in the future salvation for all Christians that God's Spirit uses to propel us in the present in order to move us continuously to steadfastness in suffering. The Spirit of God, by God's Word, strengthened this dear brother to face suffering and sorrow by the reality of Christ's atonement for his people and the inheritance he was to receive in Christ. When you face death, in that moment, what will matter to you the most? For the Christian it is always the same. First and foremost, the doctrine of justification by faith. Second, the doctrine of glorification. Those twin towers of truth are what resonate with us, God's people, in light of the shadow of trials and death itself. These twin truths are the reality that we are eternally secure in. These truths are what gave this faithful deacon hope in heartache and even propelled him forward to continue to discharge his duties as a faithful deacon. A week after that diagnosis, I went to a nursing home to visit a member of our church, another great man of God, and a deacon. As I entered into the rehab center it moved me to tears to see that another member and his wife of the church had beat me there. It was the man who weeks earlier had been diagnosed with terminal cancer and he was praying with a woman who had lost her daughter and ministering to the brother I had come to see. What propels such great service in our Lord? Nothing but the cross of Christ and what that cross brings forever!

## Eternally Secure

The area is secure! As a young kid I remember pretending to a be soldier and after examining and "taking" a new room in the home calling back to a friend that "the area is secure." We were pretending to go into hostile territory and to advance our "military might" with every soldier defeated and battlefield made secure as a part of our expanding empire. That is exactly what God is doing today as he draws his elect out of every tribe, tongue, and nation unto the Lord Jesus. He is securing his territory, namely his church, and advancing his kingdom. Peter outlines in v. 5 the absolute security of believers. He announces that his readers are "protected by the power of God through faith." Protected is a present tense participle describing the Christian state and in the original language it means "guarded, watched over."[7] These Christians are continuously guarded by the power of God through faith for "a salvation to be revealed in the last time." This salvation is the future deliverance from God's judgment against the wicked. These Christians and all Christians are kept surely from God's wrath and into God's forever family. The means of their security is God's power to give them and keep them steadfast in faith.

7. Louw, *Greek-English Lexicon*, 485.

I remember learning this doctrine (perseverance of the saints) for the first time as a new Christian. The reality that Jesus saved us forever on his cross was a beautiful delight to a soul that despaired over the ease of slipping into various sins. I remember sharing this with a lady at work who was a professing Christian. I was just green enough to think that everyone believed in Jesus saving and keeping forever his people. As I shared the wonderful news, that meant so much to me, my coworker responded, "I do not believe that. I do not believe we are eternally secure!" She later posed a question in the following terms, "So, if I go and murder someone are you saying that I'm still a Christian?" As a new believer I remember feeling stumped. It was Jesus' obedience not mine that procured my eternal destiny. That fact was the essence of the gospel, however I did not know how to respond. Yet as time goes on, Scripture becomes more clear and the faulty assumptions of that argument become increasingly grotesque. This lady assumed that a Christian could easily fall into a sin like this if they did not keep themselves straight. Also, in the argument, this lady denied God's sovereignty, though I'm sure she would not agree. Lastly, this lady assumed there were certain "sins" that would knock us out of grace. What are we to make of such an argument? One, God is sovereign over every detail of our existence. This is not something that can even be debated in Scripture, though the natural state of man rails against it. If God saves someone, is he not sovereign enough and powerful enough to keep them from various activities and sin? Second, a Christian is someone who is born again to a living hope and kept in the power of God through faith. This language implies we are a new creature. Paul states as much in 2 Corinthians 5:17 when he states, "*Therefore if anyone is in Christ, he is a new creature; the old things passed away; behold, new things have come*" (2 Cor 5:17, emphasis mine). New creatures have new desires and new actions. A person who says they are Christian yet exhibits no life change, no repentance, and enduring faith is as foolish as someone who says they just got hit by an anvil dropped on their head from the Eiffel Tower yet are unscathed. We would look at them as ludicrous. Lastly, to classify sins in categories of severe versus not so severe is not different than the Catholic doctrine of mortal sins that propels a person out of a state of grace. The error is not in the reality of varying consequences for various sins, but the assumption that some sins separate us from God's manifest presence while others do not. If we break one part of the law we break it all (Jas 2:10). Jesus fulfilled the law perfectly and we are in him and per Jesus himself, all who the Father gives to him, he will never let go of (John 10:27–30). Peter conveys the reality that God's means of guarding us for himself forever is tied to him producing in us a steadfast faith that endures to the end. For by grace we are saved through faith! By grace we are kept through faith! Those who fall away, well, John the apostle said it best "they were never of us" (1 John 2:19). Trials and tribulations, difficulties and disasters, will often sift the wheat from the tares. Trials have a way of showing whether we really believe in Jesus and are born again or not, and, at the expense of most trials, many people leave the faith and show they were never of it.

## Steadfast in Trials

There was once a man who in one day lost all his earthly wealth. He lost all his children. He lost everything of value as many today would define it. He was struck with disease that consumed his body. Was nagged and mocked by his own wife and friends. In light of all this he rejoiced in a steadfast faith in God whose love was better than life. He said in response to the horror he faced, "Though He slay me, I will hope in Him. Nevertheless I will argue my ways before Him" (Job 13:15). He wanted to come to God honestly with the question "Why?" yet his resolve was: "Though you slay, I will hope in Him." Earlier in the midst of this man's initial loss he made the following statement: "Naked I came from my mother's womb, and naked I shall return there. The Lord gave and the Lord has taken away. Blessed be the name of the Lord" (Job 1:21). This man we know as Job. His story is quite profound because of how he handled suffering. How can a person, such as

Job, say such things in the face of loss? How? Peter outlines the "how" in vv. 6–9:

> In this you greatly rejoice, even though now for a little while, if necessary, you have been distressed by various trials, so that the proof of your faith, being more precious than gold which is perishable, even though tested by fire, may be found to result in praise and glory and honor at the revelation of Jesus Christ; and though you have not seen Him, you love Him, and though you do not see Him now, but believe in Him, you greatly rejoice with joy inexpressible and full of glory, obtaining as the outcome of your faith the salvation of your souls. (1 Pet 1:6–9)

Peter boldly communicates to these precious Christians who are suffering trials for their faith that, in light of being secure in their salvation with an inheritance that is undefiled and imperishable to come, they are to not only endure trials but rejoice in the trials (per v. 6). The word rejoice is the Greek word *agalliaō* and it is an indicative verb in the present tense. The word itself in light of its composition means to continuously be overjoyed.[8] It does not mean just to be joyful, but to be extremely joyful continuously![9] The believers he is writing to are to be a people who continually and exceedingly rejoice though they are being slain and slandered.

## *The Source of Our Joy?—Jesus Is Better than Life*

What makes them so different? Have you ever heard someone say that before? Usually those words are put forth concerning a person whose life and state of mind is radically different than everyone else around them. Perhaps that different demeanor and life is appealing and attractive to the degree that others long for what that person has. Peter, in vv. 6–9, makes the case that Christians should be such people.

What is the source of the continuous great joy of the Christian that Peter writes to? Well in v. 8 Peter states, "And though you

8. Louw, *Greek-English Lexicon*, 302.

9. Louw, *Greek-English Lexicon*, 302.

have not seen Him, you love Him, and though you do not see Him now, but believe in Him" (1 Pet 1:8). It is the Jesus whom they have not seen and do not now physically see yet they love him and trust him. It is the object of these believers' faith that fills these brothers and sisters with extreme continuous joy. It is the object of these believers' faith that enables them to endure all trials and, in the trials, shows their faith to be genuine. Peter is making a profound point in vv. 6–9. He is communicating that trials work for the good of Christians' faith as their faith is refined and ultimately will result in praise and honor at the return of Jesus. Is the faith in itself what makes these Christians joyful? Not exactly. Peter is clear that though they do not now see Jesus physically they love him and trust him. Jesus, his gospel, and his glory make all types of trials not only bearable but beautiful in the fruit that comes forth eternally in the lives of those who trust Jesus in trials. As we cling to Jesus in trials and tribulation, we are communicating to the world that Jesus is better than what it (the fallen world) has to offer. We communicate that comfort cannot compare to Christ and pleasures of any kind cannot compare to the pleasures at God's right hand in Christ. We proclaim in rejoicing in trials. We proclaim that influence, fame, and long life cannot compare to the satisfaction that springs from the well of a "heart" regenerated by God's Spirit that knows Jesus and the way of the cross. Simply put trials serve the purpose of removing the things that distract our gaze on Christ and his cross. Trials will show a believer's faith is genuine as we are steadfast in suffering. Peter states being steadfast in Christ during trials puts on display the *"proof of your faith."* The word "proof" in the original language means "genuineness seen out of testing."[10] In the test of the trials of life, our faith will be shown as genuine or fraudulent. With all this in mind trials are actually a blessing from the hand of God and produce in God's people joy in the object of Jesus who alone satisfies. Trials serve to show us whether our faith is genuine and brings God much glory as Christians rejoice in the trials which communicates to the world that God's glory is more satisfying and fulfilling than anything you will find in the

10. Louw, *Greek-English Lexicon*, 674.

fallen world we sojourn through. All of this looks to the outcome of our faith being the future glorification of our bodies and souls procured by the work of Jesus on the cross. A steadfast faith is a genuine faith that lays hold of the work of Jesus to reconcile us to God and be received by God into his everlasting kingdom coming fully to a new earth. What trials are you facing today? What affects are the trials having on your life and all those around you? Is your faith being seen by all as you rejoice? Take heart by looking to Jesus and his cross. May we gaze upon him until our minds are so filled with his glory that the only thing we can do is praise and proclaim his unequal worth in this fallen world.

## What Makes Jesus Look Beautiful?

Have you ever felt swallowed up by the celebrity worship that consumes our culture today? Perhaps, you have been in line at a grocery store and found your eyes gazing at the magazine stand to see the lives of the rich and famous on display for you to envy. At that point many people may long for a life "like that one" which they equate as a life that really matters and is successful. Our culture communicates to us that young, beautiful, talented, and rich is what matters. This mind-set has even affected the church. Christians get so excited when some celebrity makes a statement about Jesus being their best friend or their guide. When famous basketball players point up to heaven after making a shot or thank God for their talents during an interview, we see that as a big deal. Up front those things are not bad. Rather, it is wonderful to hear people who are influential give God praise as the Creator and dispenser of gifts as well as the Savior of sinners. However, what makes Jesus look beautiful are the everyday followers of Jesus rejoicing in trials and tribulations. What makes Jesus truly look beautiful is not the celebrity speech or pointing to heaven after a shot. It is the Christian who has just lost a child to cancer and in the moment of that immense pain and sorrow they are able to sincerely say and squeak out, "God is good. Jesus is enough." It is the person who, in all trials and tribulations, finds their Sabbath rest in Jesus and their delight in his glory. It is easy to thank God in the high moments of life, and we should, by the way, but it is beautiful to praise him as good and enough in the lowest moments of life. Steadfastness in suffering displays that Jesus is better than life and the outcome of our faith is greater than any temporal riches, influence, fame, or fleshly pleasure. Our heavenly minded faith will proclaim the infinite worth of our King in our trials. And there is nothing more perplexing and peculiar than a people who rejoice in trials to the praise of their King. *Jesus is beautiful to his people and his people's lives in trials will show they truly believe it!*

## Peter Expounds on Rejoicing in Trials in 1 Peter 4:12–19

Perhaps at this point you are going through a fiery trial of sorts. Maybe you have cancer. Maybe you have experienced the loss of a loved one. Maybe you are enduring slander, opposition, and persecution for your faith. The Apostle Peter wrote what we call "1 Peter" to encourage Christians who were enduring trials and persecution. In 1 Peter 4:12–19 he expounds on what he said in 1 Peter 1:6–9:

> Beloved, do not be surprised at the fiery ordeal among you, which comes upon you for your testing, as though some strange thing were happening to you; but to the degree that you share the sufferings of Christ, keep on rejoicing, so that also at the revelation of His glory you may rejoice with exultation. If you are reviled for the name of Christ, you are blessed, because the Spirit of glory and of God rests on you. Make sure that none of you suffers as a murderer, or thief, or evildoer, or a troublesome meddler; but if anyone suffers as a Christian, he is not to be ashamed, but is to glorify God in this name. For it is time for judgment to begin with the household of God; and if it begins with us first, what will be the outcome for those who do not obey the gospel of God? And if it is with difficulty that the righteous is saved, what will become of the godless man and the sinner? Therefore, those also

who suffer according to the will of God shall entrust
their souls to a faithful Creator in doing what is right.
(1 Pet 4:12–19)

Notice that Peter first and foremost tells them to not be surprised
at fiery ordeals and trials for we share in the sufferings of Jesus,
meaning we, as his metaphorical body on earth, will suffer just as
our Lord did during his ministry when he was mocked, reviled,
slandered, and killed. Our suffering in our identification with Jesus
per Peter should bring great rejoicing because it shows we are truly
of Jesus and we will share in his glory as coheirs with him. We are,
as Christians, not to suffer because of our own transgressions and
sin but to suffering for following Jesus faithfully in a fallen world
and to glorify God in our identity as a Christian (Christ follower).
After Peter depicts the cleansing work of God through trials on the
church, he conveys powerfully in v. 19 that, even in the midst of
great suffering and trials, we entrust ourselves and our souls to a
faithful Creator. We put our hope in a Sovereign God who reigns
over all and his goodness, even when all we can see is darkness
and pain. We trust in the heart of a Father who crucified his Son,
who did not take a pass on experiential suffering, but rather gave
his son who suffered on the cross God's infinite wrath to bring
us, God's people, infinite delight in life everlasting with the Triune
God.

## Rejoicing in Trials

Growing up, occasionally attending a place of worship, I never
heard much about persecution, trials, and suffering. My first real
exposure to it was as a new Christian when I was twenty-three and
I heard about a famous pastor who had a brain tumor. I read an
interview where this pastor praised God for counting him worthy
to endure this trial. In the same interview he depicted how during
Thanksgiving he collapsed and woke up in a hospital bed. At the
time, he had little children and a great church. He had it all from
the American Christian dream perspective. Conference speaker

and influential pastor. Thousands listened to him deliver the Word. Yet when he talked in that interview about the moments where he struggled in his suffering, he described how he would love to see his kids raised and walk his daughter down the aisle. He described how he would love to see various things, yet he talked about comparing those "good" things to Jesus and he made the statement, "Jesus is still better than even those things." His example rocked my world in a great way. As he rejoiced in his suffering, I saw for the first time a clearer picture of the Jesus who recently had saved my soul and his worth being greater than life. This brother modeled 1 Peter 1:6–9 and 1 Peter 4:12–19 and it radically changed my view of Jesus. Jesus will be exalted the greatest not in our most "blessed" moments but the moments when darkness and despair surround us and we proclaim to the world in view of great pain and loss, "Jesus is better!" Only one who has experienced the reality of Christ and his cross can make such a boast. Only a Christian can rejoice in trials. Only a heavenly minded person with a steadfast faith will say such a thing. As weird as that will be to the world, such a people the world is not worthy of.

## Discussion Questions

1. What adjectives does Peter use to describe what is coming for all Christians?

2. What does Peter convey concerning the security of a Christian and their faith?

3. What do trials do in the life of a Christian?

4. How does God get glory as we endure in trials being heavenly minded?

# 3

# A Steadfast Faith Is Firmly Rooted in the Word of God

## 1 Peter 1:10–12

> 10 *As to this salvation, the prophets who prophesied of the grace that would come to you made careful searches and inquiries,*
>
> 11 *seeking to know what person or time the Spirit of Christ within them was indicating as He predicted the sufferings of Christ and the glories to follow.*
>
> 12 *It was revealed to them that they were not serving themselves, but you, in these things which now have been announced to you through those who preached the gospel to you by the Holy Spirit sent from heaven—things into which angels long to look.*

How do you know the god you worship is truly God? How do you know that how you worship such a God is correct? How do you know your worldview is right and healthy? The reality is that there has to be some basis for our understanding of God and how we are to approach him. Our understanding of God, or lack of belief in a god, has to have some foundation on which to build practices and principles. Today it is increasingly popular to base our idea of God on our experiences, our philosophy as human beings seeking to make sense of the world, and/or our ideas derived from our culture. However, should those things really drive our understanding of the world and how it works? It does not take a lot of effort to see that human beings are destructive, deceitful creatures. We disagree over practically everything. Just flip on any news channel for a moment to see the most recent debate or go to any website with current events and the headlines are filled with terrorism, adultery, fornication, murder, theft, hatred, racism, etc. The reality is that those things come forth from people with worldviews about a deity or their lack of belief in one. Peoples' actions follow their ideas and beliefs. Even those who do not claim to have done things in the list I just gave still know well the bitterness of envy, jealousy, prejudice, lying, slander, etc. Surely human experience, which is so clouded in our failure to see rightly and live in a way that is constructive, cannot be the basis by which we understand and worship God or assess the reality that there is a god. This is where specific revelation from God is absolutely vital and necessary. General revelation, the creation, displays things *about* God such as he is Creator and all powerful and intelligent, etc. However, general revelation *does not tell us who* God is. Only specific revelation can tell us that. That is why the Word of God is the foundation of our faith and the source of all our understanding about theology (the study of God). Peter highlights briefly the importance of the Word of God in his letter to suffering Christians in Asia. What is fascinating is God's revelation of himself and that how he is to be worshipped revolves around the person of Jesus of Nazareth.

## It Is All about Jesus!

It was Sunday and news of the empty grave was spreading. Excitement and confusion were ready companions to the disciples as they pondered the reports given by the women who had been at the tomb early Sunday morning. Two of the disciples in Luke 24 are walking on the road from Jerusalem to Emmaus. As they are progressing and in discussion, a man approaches them asking what they are discussing and despairing about. They tell this man about Jesus who was crucified and the reports that the tomb was now empty. This man responds with the following rebuke: "O foolish men and slow of heart to believe in all that the prophets have spoken! Was it not necessary for the Christ to suffer these things and to enter into His glory?" (Luke 24:25–26). Upon this rebuke this man proceeds from Moses (first five books of the Old Testament) to all the prophets (the rest of the Old Testament) to convey what the Scriptures had put forth about Jesus and his suffering in place of his people. As they get into the town, they invite this man to stay with them and when he reclined at the table and blessed the bread their eyes were opened, and they knew this man was indeed the God-Man, the Lord Jesus, himself! In this encounter these disciples were rebuked because they were slow to believe all the Old Testament's prophecies and its clear teaching on the Messiah's work to save sinners for the Triune God's glory forever. Jesus conveyed to these two disciples, who went back to the other disciples in Jerusalem, immediately, the reality that all the Old Testament is really about him. This is the same thing Peter conveys to the Christians in Asia.

Peter profoundly points out this reality in vv. 10–12:

> As to this salvation, the prophets who prophesied of the grace that *would come* to you made careful searches and inquiries, seeking to know what person or time the Spirit of Christ within them was indicating as He predicted the sufferings of Christ and the glories to follow. It was revealed to them that they were not serving themselves, but you, in these things which now have been announced to you through those who preached the gospel to you by the Holy Spirit sent from heaven—things into which angels long to look. (1 Pet 1:10–12)

Peter states that the prophets themselves did not understand all that God's Spirit was indicating to them concerning the sufferings of Christ and the glories to follow, yet they were not ultimately writing for themselves, but for the church. What a profound statement. It fits just alongside Jesus saying to his disciples in Luke 10:23b–24, "Blessed *are* the eyes which see the things you see, for I say to you, that many prophets and kings wished to see the things which you see, and did not see *them*, and to hear the things which you hear, and did not hear *them*." What the disciples were hearing and the truth being entrusted to them were things which kings and prophets from the Old Testament longed desperately to fully comprehend and hear. Peter points out in vv. 11–12 that these prophets were "seeking to know," which is the Greek word *eraunaō* and is a participle in the active voice and present tense. Peter, in using this word in such a way, conveys that the prophets actively were pondering and continuously meditating on what the Spirit of God was inspiring them to put forth concerning the Messiah and his sufferings in order to save God's people. These prophets joined the angels in heaven (who are finite creatures learning about God as well), longing to see the fulfillment and understand the things which God's Spirit inspired. God moved the prophets of the Old Testament to pen categories, prophecies, and commands that ultimately find their fulfilment in Jesus of Nazareth. Peter also alludes to what we consider our New Testament when he states, ". . . in these things which now have been announced to you *through those who preached the gospel to you by the Holy Spirit* sent from heaven" (1 Pet 1:12, emphasis mine). Peter and the apostles proclaimed the gospel message entrusted to them by Jesus and it was the fulfillment of all the Old Testament put forth (Eph 2:19–20). Though not directly referencing the New Testament to be canonized in the hundreds of years to come, he puts the principle forth regarding what the New Testament is. It is the apostles' teaching of Jesus which fulfills the Old Testament covenant. This means that the primary purpose of the law and all of the Old Testament was to be a tutor to lead us to Jesus (Gal 3:24). This also means the New Testament, which for a book to be included had to have an apostle or an associate of an apostle as its author, is all about the person, ministry, work, resurrection, ascension, people, and return of the

Lord Jesus. Putting all this together paints a beautiful picture of the whole Bible. For the Old and New Testament is all about Jesus to the glory of God the Father inspired by God the Spirit. The Bible has commands and to-dos. The Bible has instructions and precepts. It does have commands and they are important. However, the Bible is not primarily a book of commands or to-dos. It is a book about Jesus. Angels and the redeemed alike, as finite creatures are coming to understand the grace and salvation given to the church as we see and understand Jesus from all the Bible.

## Basic Instructions Before Leaving Earth (B.I.B.L.E.)?

It was a multidenominational church service. The speaker's topic at the close of service, the Word of God. The premise of the exhortation was that the Bible is the Basic Instructions Before Leaving Earth. As the preacher expounded his position that the Bible was God's rule book, and guide to a great and abundant life, it sat rather wrongly. However, many people see the Bible as just that. They see it as primarily an instruction manual. A list of to-dos to please God and acquire his favor. While the Bible most certainly has commands and regulations, that is not the Scriptures' purpose. Per 1 Peter 2:10–12, the Bible is all about God's glory fully manifested in God the Son's incarnation, life, crucifixion, resurrection, and return. The Old Testament gives us the categories to understand God's glory in redeeming sinners and the New Testament fills those categories in the person of Jesus of Nazareth. The Bible is not the basic instructions before leaving earth. The Bible is not even primarily a love letter from God to us. The Bible (Old and New Testament) is all about Jesus and God's glory in the work of Jesus. Now before we look at the concept of following Jesus, we need to take a step back and just think on what the great gift of Holy Scripture is to us, God's creation, who have fallen. Per Ephesians 2:1–3 and Romans 1:18–32, apart from God's grace we are spiritually dead and unable to see God's glory. We would know nothing of what God is like and who he is if he had not come to us and revealed himself to us. He reveals himself to us specifically through his Word. This is why Paul in Romans 10:15 states, "How will they preach unless they are sent? Just as it is written, 'How beautiful are the feet of those who bring good news of good things!'" How beautiful are those who bring the Word of God to those who do not have it! Without the good news encased in the Word of God (both Testaments), people can never know God through faith in Jesus. God's Word is the foundation of the church which God uses to build his church by his Holy Spirit.

## The Word of God (Old and New Testament) by the Spirit of God Makes the People of God

Peter in vv. 10–12 makes it clear that salvation is understood only from the writings of the prophets, who continuously toiled over what the Spirit of God had inspired them to put forth concerning the person and work of Jesus, as well as what the apostles preached and taught. If truth of Jesus is found solely in the Bible, then logically, the Bible is what the church is built on. This reality is what Jesus conveyed to his disciples after he asked them who everyone was saying he was in Matthew 16. Jesus, in response to Peter's confession that he (Jesus) is the Christ, the Son of God, in Matthew 16, states the following:

> And Jesus said to him, "Blessed are you, Simon Barjona, because flesh and blood did not reveal this to you, but My Father who is in heaven. I also say to you that you are Peter, and upon this rock I will build My church; and the gates of Hades will not overpower it. I will give you the keys of the kingdom of heaven; and whatever you bind on earth shall have been bound in heaven, and whatever you loose on earth shall have been loosed in heaven." (Matt 16:17–19)

Jesus tells Peter in v. 18 that he (Jesus) will build the church and he tells Peter that upon this "rock" he will do it. What is the rock? Some organizations have interpreted that rock to be Peter himself, however it is clear in Peter's writings that he did not share their view (1 Pet 2:7). Nor did any of the other apostles view Peter in such terms (Eph 2:20). So . . . who or what is the rock? I believe the key to unlocking that door is what follows in the rest of the passage. In v. 19 Jesus tells Peter that he gives to him the keys of the kingdom and those keys unlock and bind. What are those keys? It is clear those keys unlock heaven for people. Therefore . . . it is not Saint Peter sitting by some heavenly gate, for that would contradict all inspired Scripture (Eph 2:8–10; John 14:6; Rom 10:9, etc.), rather it was what Jesus entrusted to Peter and all the apostles. Jesus entrusted his gospel (*the gospel being Jesus who is fully God and sinless man dying on the cross in the stead of sinners and rising on the third day validating for all time his identity and work on the cross to reconcile sinners to a Holy God*) and all its implications in the new covenant to the apostles. Now this new covenant *revolves around what Peter confessed—Jesus as the Messiah and Son of God.* Jesus is saying that on his Word, which he entrusted to the apostles, he was going to build his church. *Think about it. For a book to be included in the New Testament it had to have an apostle or an associate of an apostle as its source.*

## The Word of God Rightly Proclaimed Builds Churches and Christians

Jesus inspired the apostles by his Holy Spirit to convey his teachings entrusted to them. That is the point Paul makes in Ephesians 2:19–22: "So then you are no longer strangers and aliens, but you are fellow citizens with the saints, and are of God's household, having been built on the foundation of the apostles and prophets, Christ Jesus Himself being the corner stone, in whom the whole building, being fitted together, is growing into a holy temple in the Lord, in whom you also are being built together into a dwelling of God in the Spirit." In this text, Paul describes what the household of God (which is where the Spirit of God indwells, per vv. 19 and 22) is built on. The household of God, with the Spirit of God indwelling (temple imagery), is Paul's depiction of the church because only the people of God are indwelled by the Spirit of God. Notice he says that the church is built, it is made on the foundation of the apostles and prophets with Jesus as the cornerstone. The cornerstone was the chief stone from which all the other stones lined up. All of Scripture, both New and Old Testaments, points to Jesus. The Scripture rightly preached, taught, explained, and applied is what Jesus uses to bring forth his people out of this world and build them up in faith and holiness. Jesus builds his church and Christians through the apostolic teachings he entrusted to his disciples. He builds his church through the faithful sharing and proclamation of the Bible.

If this is true, then a faithful church and Christian will be marked by biblical soundness and faithfulness. A faithful church (a group of believers that assemble, not a building) will, Sunday after Sunday, examine the Scripture in light of its literal historical context to mine out God's timeless truths, which exalt the gospel of Christ. A faithful church/Christian will conduct itself per God's Word rightly interpreted and proclaim God's Word rightfully divided. A faithful church/Christian will proclaim the Word of God to the world and engage in the mission of God the way the Word of God communicates. A faithful church/Christian will not be marked by "I/we have always done it this way." A faithful church/Christian will be marked by examining all things considering "what does Scripture say rightly interpreted?" Inevitably, we must ask ourselves the hard question: Am I a person who has built my life on the shifting sands of topics (even professed Christian ones), opinions, and cultural philosophies of my context? *Or is my* life built on the foundation of the apostles and prophets, namely the Word of God? Is my view of the world shaped by God's Word rightly interpreted (understanding it in light of its literal, historical, grammatical context)? Only one foundation (the Word of God) will keep the house standing in the storms of life. Jesus builds his church on the rock of the Word. Is it any wonder that dear saints have died willingly in defense of translation of the Scriptures so that people may have its truth?

## *William Tyndale's Love of the Word*

William Tyndale was proficient in languages, as a matter of fact he could speak seven different languages. He was diligent in Greek and Hebrew and as a priest had access to Erasmus's Greek New Testament. In that work, Tyndale discovered the doctrine of justification by faith alone, in Christ alone. Upon such an awakening it became his personal goal, as he told one Catholic who defended the pope's decrees over God's precepts, that with translating the Bible into English it was his desire to see all English speakers given access to the Word of God. He stated, "I defy the Pope and all his laws. If God spare my life, ere many years I will cause a boy who drives the plough to know more of the Scriptures than you do." Tyndale would be strangled and burned at the stake for his work to get the Scriptures into the hands of all people who spoke English.[1] The Word of God which housed the person of Jesus of Nazareth was worth dying for. Amazingly enough, the English world would have a Bible to put into the hands of every person and would be the hub of evangelical missionary activity for approximately two hundred plus years. What Tyndale died for paid eternal dividends to God's praise among all peoples. The Word of God is alive and active.

## What the Bible Says about Itself

What do you have to say for yourself!? Normally when a person hears that, he or she has done something that warrants an explanation, whether good or bad. The idea is explaining why these results that are readily evident have occurred. The Bible actually goes to great length to explain itself in many places. One of the best examples is found in Paul's Second Letter to Timothy. Paul, describing the Old Testament Scriptures, which has the same implications for the New Testament in 2 Timothy 3:16–17, states, "All Scripture is inspired by God and profitable for teaching, for reproof, for correction, for training in righteousness; so that the man of God may

1. Galli and Olsen, *131 Christians*, 348–50.

be adequate, equipped for every good work." The term "inspire" comes from the Latin, "to breathe in," and it is misleading with regards to understanding this verse. The actual Greek term for "inspired" is *theopneustos* and it means God breathed out.[2] It is God breathing out his revelation of himself through the Words of human authors. God breathed out his Word through his moving human authors to convey his timeless truth in their culture, situation, and with their personality and writing style. The Bible is God's Word conveyed through human instruments. Peter put it this way in his second epistle, "But know this first of all, that no prophecy of Scripture is *a matter* of one's own interpretation, for no prophecy was ever made by an act of human will, *but men moved by the Holy Spirit spoke from God*" (2 Pet 1:20–21, emphasis mine). The authority the Scripture claims for itself is profound. The Bible does not hide the fact that it is the truth from God himself. It is the only way to know God himself and to worship God rightly. The defining qualities of the God we worship and how we approach him matter. We as fallen creatures cannot see those things in our unredeemed state. Therefore, God gives his Word which, by his Spirit, moves us to know him and worship him. As Jesus said in John 4, "God is spirit, and those who worship Him must worship in spirit and truth" (John 4:24). We must be born again by the Holy Spirit and worship God as he revealed himself in his truth which is only found in his Word. The Bible depicts this process of illuminating mankind's mind and understanding in places like Psalm 119 and Hebrews 4:12. God's Word makes the claim that it is the only true revelation of God. And for those who may think 2 Timothy 3:16 and others do not apply to the New Testament, the New Testament intrinsically makes claims about itself. Peter considers the letters of Paul inspired in 2 Peter 3:15–16. Paul treats a quotation from the Gospel of Luke as inspired Scripture, citing Luke 10:7 in 1 Timothy 5:18. Revelation is adamant about its own inspiration in Revelation 22:18–19. Paul was aware that he was writing with divine authority in 1 Corinthians 2:12; 1 Corinthians 14:37; Galatians 1:11–12; 1 Thessalonians 2:13. The Bible is not one holy book

2. Swanson, *Dictionary of Biblical Languages*, s.v. "theopneustos."

among many. It is the only book that reveals God specifically, for in it you find Jesus alone (John 14:6). The rest are counterfeits from the imaginations of fallen mankind.

## Well . . . Why Are Certain Books Included?

Have you ever wondered how the books of the Bible were recognized? Did they put all the names in the proverbial hat and just pick them out and then put those books in the canon of Scripture? The *Lexham Bible Dictionary* outlines the criteria for how a book was recognized in the New Testament canon as the following:

- Apostolicity, meaning it was written by an apostle or someone closely associated with an apostle.

- Orthodoxy, meaning it was considered in line with the "rule of faith"—core Christian beliefs as taught by the apostles and in accord with the Old Testament writings.

- Catholicity, meaning it gained widespread acceptance throughout Christendom.

- Traditional usage, meaning it was read as Scripture in public worship and discussed in Christian literature as Scripture.

- Antiquity, meaning it was written as close as possible to the original events.

- Officialization, meaning it became part of an official collection.[3]

In essence, what the *Lexham Dictionary* shows is that all New Testament books must have an apostle or an associate of an apostle as the author, be universally recognized by the church, and be consistent with the rule of faith (the apostles' teaching). This very criterion eliminates books fraudulently assigned to various figures such as the *Gospel of Thomas* or the *Gospel of Mary*. The New

---

3. *Lexham Bible Dictionary*, s.v. "Canon, New Testament" (entry written by S. T. Raquel).

Testament canon is closed and complete and was universally accepted by the church.

## How about the Old Testament?

The Old Testament canon was collected over a long period as well and universally recognized by the people of God. The criteria for canonization and the acceptance of it by Jesus as inspired by God in all thirty-nine books that it consists of makes a strong case that it is the complete Old Testament revelation of God. Books such as the Apocrypha are rejected from being included in the Old Testament because they do not claim for themselves authority as the Old Testament writings do; they were not regarded as God's Word by the Jewish people from whom they originated; they were not considered part of Holy Scripture per Jesus or the New Testament writers; and they contain teachings inconsistent with both the Old and New Testament.[4] The Old Testament canon has to agree with the revealed counsel of God and have been universally accepted by the Jewish people. The criteria for canonization for both the New and Old Testament give us confidence that we have the complete set, with all the books that God truly has inspired.[5]

# Is the Bible Accurately Transmitted?

Now before we proceed, at this point we need to go back to theme of the opening of this chapter. The Word of God is about God's glory fully manifested in Jesus. It shows us who God is, who we are, and how we can only worship him through the work of Jesus (John 14:6). It claims to be from God. Now, how do we know that what the Old Testament (written primarily in Hebrew with a little Aramaic in there) and New Testament (written in Greek) says about Jesus is reliable and has been preserved since it was penned

4. Grudem, *Systematic Theology*, 59–60.

5. For more information on this topic, books like Wayne Grudem's *Systematic Theology* or F. F. Bruce's *Canon of Scripture* are especially helpful.

thousands of years ago? Perhaps this is a question you have thought of or even been approached with by an unbeliever. This has been a point of contention with many skeptics in the region I pastor. They claim the Bible has been translated repeatedly to the point, like the game telephone, we have lost the original message. If you have ever played telephone, you know that you start with a statement and then communicate that to someone who communicates it to someone with the end result being that the ending message does not even resemble the beginning message. Many skeptics claim that same principle with the transmission of the Bible. Is that accurate? How do we know that the Bible we have was the very words Peter, Paul, James, Moses, etc., put forth? The answer is the art and science of textual criticism. Let us take the New Testament for example for that is the area that receives much attention.

Getting to the original wording of Scripture by examining the manuscripts of the Old Testament and New Testament is textual criticism. A manuscript is a copy of the original. It is obviously several copies removed from the first text. With Old Testament manuscripts, it is estimated that there are tens of thousands.[6] Per certain counts, there are approximately 5,812 New Testament Greek manuscripts.[7] There are over 10,000 Latin manuscripts of the New Testament as well, which is helpful in seeing how the Greek was translated in the first several centuries of the early church.[8] Textual Criticism compares the manuscripts to produce the original wording of the original authors. The question is, then, how close do we get to the originals through textual criticism. Apologist Norman Geisler states the following:

> In short, the NT is 98.33 percent pure. Second, Greek expert Ezra Abbott said about 19/20 (95 percent) of the readings are "various" rather than "rival" readings, and about 19/20 (95 percent) of the rest make no appreciable difference in the sense of the passage. Thus the text is

6. Geisler, *General Introduction to the Bible*, 356–58.

7. *Lexham Bible Dictionary*, s.v. "Textual Criticism of the New Testament" (entry written by D. B. Wallace).

8. *Lexham Bible Dictionary*, s.v. "Textual Criticism of the New Testament."

99.75 percent accurate. Third, noted NT Greek scholar A. T. Robertson said the real concern is with about a "thousandth part of the entire text." So, the reconstructed text of the New Testament is 99.9% free from real concern.

Philip Schaff estimated that of the thousands of variations in all the manuscripts known in his day, only 50 were of real significance and of these not one affected "an article of faith." Even agnostic NT critic Bart Ehrman admits that *"In fact, most of the changes found in early Christian manuscripts have nothing to do with theology or ideology.* Far and away the most changes are the result of mistakes pure and simple-slips of the pen, accidental omissions, inadvertent additions, misspelled words, blunders of one sort or another" (*Misquoting Jesus*, 55).[9]

What this means for us is that when you and I read great translations like the ESV, NASB, CSB, etc., we are reading translations that are based on the very words of the apostles and their associates. Your Bible is reliable, which confronts us with the reality of a God who is Holy, man who is spiritually dead, and a Savior who brings a people to a Holy God forever through his righteousness.[10]

The Bibles (the faithful translations) we read are accurately and completely transmitted. These translations carry the same authority and inerrancy with them if the translation carries the original meaning of the original authors. The Bible is God's Word, inspired by the person of the Holy Spirit as he moved men to write in their context. This makes the Bible God's only specific revelation to us. God's revelation is primarily about his glory manifested in the Lord Jesus.

---

9. Geisler, "Note of the Percent of Accuracy."

10. For more information on this topic, books like Timothy Paul Jones's *Misquoting Truth* and F. F. Bruce's *Are the New Testament Documents Reliable* are of great benefit.

## The Implications of the Doctrine of the Bible

To know Jesus is to know God the Father. All the Bible is primarily about Jesus. The Bible is God's Word for all time, and we know it has been accurately collected (the canon) and transmitted from the original manuscripts. Therefore, we have to wrestle with, and come to terms with what we read in its passages. *The implication of this is if we want to know Jesus more and savor him in a greater way then we need to know all of the Bible.* We need to systematically read it and interpret it in light of its literal, historical, and grammatical context. We must be a people of the Word if we claim to be a people who love Jesus. We cannot separate the two. We need to have the same hunger as the prophets of the Old Testament when Peter described them per vv. 10–12, "As to this salvation, the prophets who prophesied of the grace that *would come* to you *made careful searches and inquiries, seeking to know what person or time the Spirit of Christ within them was indicating as he predicted the sufferings of Christ and the glories to follow.* It was revealed to them that they were not serving themselves, but you, in these things which now have been announced to you through those who preached the gospel to you by the Holy Spirit sent from heaven—things into which angels long to look" (1 Pet 1:10–12, emphasis mine). We must hit the rock of the Word with diligent study as they did till we see the water of life flow clearly from it. We must be diligent to study the Word of God. For it has always been the spark that has created a fire for God's glory. Luther, whose love of Scripture and its doctrine fanned into flame the Reformation which reclaimed the gospel, said this during his early years of Bible study: "With great loathing I read physics [Arisotle's Physics], and my heart was aglow when the time came to return to the Bible. . . . I read the Bible diligently. Sometimes one statement occupied all my thoughts for a whole day."[11] Amazing how Luther's love for the Scripture mirrored the prophets before him, and as he beat the tree of Scripture diligently in study for the fruits that hung there,

---

11. Sproul, *Legacy of Luther*, 98.

what fell was the fruit of the gospel which brought him life. No less is needed today in the Western church.

## Discussion Questions

1. What is the Bible?

2. What is the Bible primarily about?

3. How do we know the Bible we hold is accurate and the very Word of God?

4. What implications does the Bible being God's inerrant, infallible Word have for us today?

# 4

## A Steadfast Faith Reflects the Character of God Increasingly in the Present

### 1 Peter 1:13–21

13 *Therefore, prepare your minds for action, keep sober in spirit, fix your hope completely on the grace to be brought to you at the revelation of Jesus Christ.*

14 *As obedient children, do not be conformed to the former lusts which were yours in your ignorance,*

15 *but like the Holy One who called you, be holy yourselves also in all your behavior;*

16 *because it is written, "You shall be holy, for I am holy."*

17 *If you address as Father the One who impartially judges according to each one's work, conduct yourselves in fear during the time of your stay on earth;*

18 *knowing that you were not redeemed with perishable things like silver or gold from your futile way of life inherited from your forefathers,*

19 *but with precious blood, as of a lamb unblemished and spotless, the blood of Christ.*

20 *For He was foreknown before the foundation of the world, but has appeared in these last times for the sake of you*

21 *who through Him are believers in God, who raised Him from the dead and gave Him glory, so that your faith and hope are in God.*

MOST KIDS KNOW THE game Follow the Leader. The idea of the game is to mimic the behavior, sounds, and statements the leader makes. If the leader jumps then all the followers are to jump. If the leader yells, "Wow!" all are to yell, "Wow!" This game can get out of hand quickly, especially if the leader is a bit eccentric and creative. However, as an adult it is rather fun to watch a bunch of kids mimicking a high-energy, agile, and quick-witted kid. It is definitely something that makes you stop and look. A Christian is a follower of Jesus and because he purchased us from God the Father's wrath we are called to mimic his character and convey his words to a world that should stop and look at what is perceived as peculiar behavior. Peter, beginning in v. 13, exhorts us to fix our hope on Jesus (v. 13) and his grace which produces a life that follows our Leader, who is holy (vv. 15–16). Peter reminds us the reason we follow this Leader is because he shed his blood to redeem us (vv. 17–21). The cost of our redemption was the infinitely valuable blood of the Lamb of God, and because we belong to Jesus, he is refining us to reflect back to him his communicable characteristics.

## A "Therefore" Followed by Five "To Dos"

The word "therefore" is often skipped over as we read, not only in the Bible, but in other literature. However, this word has great importance. It is a word that connects what the author has just previously said with what the author will say next. Peter begins v. 13 with the word "therefore," which is the Greek word *dio*, conveying that the salvation God has brought about in these Christians' lives is the basis from which they are to obey the commands in the following verses from vv. 13–16. Peter is saying that because God has caused you to be born again to living hope, which Christ secured by his resurrection, you are commanded in the present to live a certain way. The fact of Jesus saving these people for all time is followed by the commands of Jesus to live out in the present time, not to earn salvation, but to magnify the One who gave salvation completely for all eternity. The way Peter describes how they should live is seen in two commands and three participles. The two commands are: "fix your hope completely" (v. 13) and "be holy" (v. 15). The three participle phrases are: "prepare your minds for action" (v. 13), "keep sober in spirit" (v. 13), and "do not be conformed to the former lusts" (v. 14). The three participles either support the commands or they take the role of commands as seen in the NIV.[1] Regardless, the exhortations of all five of these phrases are items we, as born-again believers in the present, are to practice. Therefore, let us take a moment to analyze each of the five exhortations that Peter gives concerning the implications for the born-again Christians' everyday life.

## (1) Prepare Your Minds for Action and (2) Keep Sober in Spirit

"Wherefore gird up the loins of your mind" is how the King James Version translates "Therefore, prepare your minds for action" (1 Pet 1:13). While the King James is not my favorite choice of translation, its conveyance of the original in this way is very accurate. Peter uses the word *anazōnnymi* which means gird up. One commentator described what Peter meant here in the following way: "The image of 'girding up the loins' (*anazōsamenoi tas osphyas*) means that one tucks in one's long flowing garments to run or do serious work."[2] The idea Peter wants these believers in Asia to grasp ahold of is they need to be disciplined in their thinking. He follows up this exhortation with the second exhortation, "Keep

1. Raymer, "1 Peter," 842–43.
2. Schreiner, *1, 2 Peter, Jude*, 78.

sober in spirit" in v. 13, which furthers Peter's call for these Christians to be clear-minded and filled with truth. When you hear the word "sober" does your mind immediately go to someone who has, for a good while, not had a drink of alcohol? That is where most people's minds tend to go. Peter, in v. 13, tells his readers to "keep sober in spirit." "Keep sober" is the Greek word *nēphō* and is a participle in the present tense. The word in its construction means to continuously be clear-headed.[3] The phrase "keep sober" originally meant abstaining from excessive use of wine, but in the New Testament it broadens to include embracing sound judgment in all areas of life.[4] Peter calls these Christians to be clear-headed and disciplined in filling their minds with truth. They need not spend all their mental energy on useless and worthless things. Paul said it this way in Philippians 4:8: "Finally, brethren, whatever is true, whatever is honorable, whatever is right, whatever is pure, whatever is lovely, whatever is of good repute, if there is any excellence and if anything worthy of praise, dwell on these things." Paul, like Peter, calls for those redeemed by Jesus to gird up their minds by being disciplined in their thinking. To dwell on the truth of God's Word, his works, his glory, and his kingdom to fully come. We are not to allow our minds to dwell continuously on trivial and unworthy items. Why would Peter be so concerned with these Christians' thoughts and minds, and thereby our minds as well? Why is this the first exhortation?

My youngest son loves dinosaurs. He talks about them all the time and reads about them habitually. When we are out and about at the store, he asks for this dinosaur toy or that. He pretends to be a dinosaur and will even chase his sisters around the house as if he is a T-Rex who is looking for its next victim. My son's behavior is indicative of what he thinks about. His fascination with dinosaurs leads to his asking for dinosaur toys, pretending to be a dinosaur, and talking about dinosaurs all the time. What we think about the most will come out in our petitions, lifestyle, and conversations. When we fill our minds with the truth of God's Word, God's

---

3. Swanson, *Dictionary of Biblical Languages*, s.v. "nēphō."

4. Barker, "1 Peter," in *Expositor's Bible Commentary*, 1045.

truth is continually before us. When our minds are continuously consumed with his glory in our lives, in the power of the Holy Spirit, we begin to look more and more like the Lord Jesus that we profess to follow. The Spirit sanctifies us by the Word (John 17:17; Rom 12:2). Therefore, Peter exhorts Christians to "prepare our minds for action." To be disciplined in our thinking. In today's entertainment-driven culture, Christians need to, more than ever, heed these words.

In many circles it is poplar to base sermon structure and even length based on the perceived attention span of those in attendance and especially seekers. Now up front, I'm not for long sermons just for the sake of long sermons, and I believe strongly that boring preaching is sin for it lies about God. God is not boring therefore preaching should not be. The concern over people's attention span centers around a belief that people do not have the mental capacity to handle longer or more in-depth, expositional messages. However, in the context of the church this cannot be the whole story. Students will sit and solve difficult problems in calculus, chemistry, and literature. Adults will labor over complex issues at work. Yet when it comes to church we do not expect them to be able to really go into depth theologically or dig deep expositionally. Members can most certainly watch movies, their favorite baseball or basketball team, and favorite shows for hours on end and not get "bored." What is the issue? It is an issue of what we love to think about. As Calvin once conveyed in his *Institutes of the Christian Religion* (my paraphrase), "The human heart is an idol factory."[5] The lack of willingness to engage in preaching beyond a certain time frame or level of depth is a misplaced love issue. The pastor must be diligent, of course, to prepare expositional, engaging messages well, but the church must "prepare their minds for action" by being a people who hunger for, think on, and apply the Word of God. Our favorite baseball teams, movies, and shows should not be what consumes the majority of our minds and thoughts. Our lack of discipline for the Word shows our lack of love for the Lord Jesus. In our entertainment- and social media–driven society, this

5. Calvin, *Institutes*, 54.

is increasingly difficult to convey. It is important to remember that the glory of God is seen in the pages of Scripture. As Christians, we are to gird up the loins of our minds and study the Word rightly divided, every day. We do this not to stay saved or earn salvation or even to be a "good" Christian. We do this because we are forever and completely forgiven and redeemed by the finished work of Jesus (1 Pet 1:1–12). Therefore, as the redeemed, we long for his kingdom and increasingly love and enjoy him. We do this because thinking on Jesus is increasingly our delight, not our drudge-filled duty.

## (3) Fix Your Hope Completely on the Grace to be Brought at the Revelation of Jesus

Peter tells these beloved believers to "fix their hope completely on the grace to be brought." The phrase "to be brought" is a participle in the present tense and conveys that the grace and kindness of God that will be given to God's people at the return of Jesus is continuous and unending. God's kindness that comes with the kingdom of God fully-realized does not cease or ever end. Peter gives a command to these Christians to look toward and fix their hope on the unending kindness of God that will come to us at the return of Jesus. Why would Peter tell these Christians during present tense exhortations to move their focus to the kingdom to come? Have you ever noticed how easy it is to lose perspective? To miss the forest for the trees. For example, people will get so worked up about current issues in their job, with their peers, or regarding various friends, betrayals, etc., that they lose focus on what really matters and is important.

I'm not a TV series watcher by any means but I have stumbled on a show that I find is fascinating called *Downton Abbey*. What makes this show interesting is that it portrays a wealthy aristocratic class in England and the domestic workers under them as that era came to an end. The TV show centers around the Crawley family who live in this mansion and have been caretakers of the property for generations. Those who work for the Crawleys are numerous and they have various reporting structures. However, all the workers report up to Mr. Carson. The show does a fantastic job of showing how each of these workers plots, worries about, plans, and conceives various ways to get ahead in the house and move up into better positions in the Crawley home, called "Downton Abbey." As you progress, it becomes clear what they worried about or plotted to get really didn't matter much nor did it bring them joy. It was meaningless. They missed the forest of living a life of eternal value for the trees of position, influence, approval, and comfort. This story is not confined to Downton Abbey. This is the story of mankind in our fallen nature. We, by nature, live for things that will burn up forever and as Christians it is easy to fall back again into that way of thinking. Therefore, Peter calls these Christians to cast their gaze beyond the individual trees of trials and tribulations before them to ultimately fix their eyes on the forest of God's grace to come to them when the Lord Jesus returns. To live in light of the hope of Christ's imminent return. The concept of hope that Peter uses corresponds to Paul's usage of faith, for hope is a trust in God for the fulfillment of all his promises to be realized in the future.[6] God has promised to bring his people into perfection. To perfect their souls and bodies and to give them a perfect place to dwell forever with a perfect and pure King. The phrase "the revelation of Jesus Christ" at the end of v. 13 is the exact phrase Peter used at the end of v. 7 after he had described the inheritance and living hope believers have to look forward to. The point is clear. Peter calls believers to fix their focus, to trust wholly the promises of God to be fulfilled in the new heavens and earth that are coming at the return of the Lord Jesus. Having that focus helps us to evaluate our present and be sober and disciplined with what we think on and live for.

6. Schreiner, *1, 2 Peter, Jude*, 77.

## So What Does This Mean?

So what? If you are the parent of a teenager, maybe you have heard these words. Usually after having conveyed something important, you are met back with the words, "So what?" However, even if teenagers mean it disrespectfully, it is still a logical and great response. We need to ask, "So what?" concerning what these three exhortations mean for our everyday lives. These three exhortations go together and have great meaning for our lives today. For example, if you are working in an office as an accountant, your ultimate focus is not moving up to this or that position, to work and connive to that end, but rather to work hard to the glory of God (1 Cor 10:31; 1 Pet 2:19). You realize that ultimately the company and the position and the comforts that come forth from these things will perish, but what is done for the glory of God in your workplace and with your social structure will last forever. Instead of spending all our time being entertained in our entertainment-saturated culture, we will diligently spend time with God in his Word, prayer, and the like. When our focus is on the promises of God to be fulfilled fully in Jesus we will not be obsessed with sports teams and stats that have very little eternal value in contrast with the unreached peoples who lack access to the gospel as well as the orphan, AIDS, and various other health crises around the world that call for our attention and engagement. Stepping outside our personal struggles and issues to see clearly the forest of God's glory moves us to live in the present in a vastly different way with drastically different motives and mind-sets.

## (4) Do Not Be Conformed to the Former Lusts and (5) Be Holy

Peter reminds these Christians in Asia Minor that they are to be obedient "children" who no longer live in their past ignorance. He calls them to live holy lives in line with the character of the Holy God they now call Father. Peter states, "As obedient children, do not be conformed to the former lusts *which were yours* in your

ignorance, but like the Holy One who called you, be holy yourselves also in all *your* behavior; because it is written, 'You shall
be holy, for I am holy'" (1 Pet 1:14–16). Here Peter reminds these
believers of their new identity which Jesus has procured for them
in his cross. He calls them "obedient children" in v. 14 and as God's
children we are not to act as we once did when we lived in moral
and spiritual darkness. He reminds them of their former ignorance, which, by the way, is a strong piece of evidence these are
Gentile converts for Jews were not ignorant of the law. Peter calls
them forth to continuously refuse to live like they used to. "Do
not be conformed" is a participle phrase in the present tense and
it means to not continually align their behavior with their former
values. Peter here is strongly commending these Christians to not
act like they did when they lived; ignorant of God and his glory.
One commentator stated about Peter's view of the present in light
of the believers' past and future salvation that he had already put
forth, "They are God's children, and as his children they are to
obey him. We have already seen that obedience is necessary for
conversion and cannot, ultimately, be separated from faith, though
it flows from faith. *Peter had no conception of the Christian life in
which believers give mere mental assent to doctrines.*"[7] Peter then
moves to the positive aspects of behavior that they are to live out.
He reminds them of who God is in the opening words of v. 15
when he describes God the Father as the "Holy One." Now at this
point we need to stop a moment and think about what that means.

## God Is Holy and We Are to Be Holy

One of the greatest chapters in all the Bible to see what is meant
by the phrase "Holy One" is Isaiah 6. In Isaiah 6, Isaiah is taken
up, most likely in a vision, to the throne room of God where God's
glory is brightly on display as Isaiah sees God on his throne, highly
exalted and praised. Isaiah sees angles praising God, saying in Isaiah 6:3, "And one called out to another and said, '*Holy, Holy, Holy,*

7. Schreiner, *1, 2 Peter, Jude*, 79.

*is the Lord of hosts, The whole earth is full of His glory'"*(Isa 6:3, emphasis mine). The focus of what the angels are saying to God in praise is *"Holy, Holy, Holy."* Holy meaning "separate" or "other." God is separate from his creation. He is in a category all by himself. God is the greatest and most glorious of all beings. He is eternal and unchanging. He is all-powerful and fully everywhere at all times. He is all-knowing and a Triune Being. He is perfectly pure, just, compassionate, and merciful. He is love. God transcends time and space. His plans cannot be thwarted, and his decrees always come to pass. He does all things for his glory, for he upholds himself as the greatest of all beings, infinitely greater than the most beautiful created thing (Isa 42:8). God is holy! Peter reminds these Christians of the God they now belong to as children and who he is. Then he quotes from Leviticus 11:44 (and other Old Testament passages) where the author conveys the Lord saying, "Be holy, for I am holy" (Lev 11:44). In Leviticus God followed that up with, "You shall not make yourselves unclean" (Lev 11:44), and then lists a dietary restriction. The idea of being holy as God is holy, in its Old Testament context, means being a people who were in a separate category from the world. The people of God where to reflect, on a finite, basis God's holiness by being separate in their minds, affections, and actions from the fallen world-system around them. It is precisely that meaning that Peter is applying to the Christians in Asia when he issues the command "to be holy in your behavior" (1 Pet 1:15). In setting his heart on us, setting us apart by the Holy Spirit to faith in Jesus in the past, God is bringing to our lives a present pattern that is different than the sin-saturated world around us. As we look to the future to come for God's people, we encouraged in the present to be holy and forsake sin. We are to live lives in a different category of standards than the world around us! We are to follow our leader and mimic his character as his people.

# I Thought I Would Be More Sanctified by Now

Do these types of commands discourage you? For many Christians who know well their struggles and failings, it can. If you have been a Christian for any length of time you may have had the following thought cross your mind, "I thought I would be more sanctified by now. I thought I would resemble Jesus more." As we follow Christ, we struggle with the presence of a sin nature that has not been taken away. The power of sin is broken, yes. However, its presence remains. We are a torn people. We hear Peter's five exhortations and a part of us craves to follow them and another part resists. We are new creatures in Christ with new desires, yet we still have some of the old that lingers around. We are a people who know well the struggle of the flesh and the Holy Spirit. Paul highlights this internal war within the Christian in Galatians 5:16–26, as he states:

> But I say, walk by the Spirit, and you will not carry out the desire of the flesh. For the flesh sets its desire against the Spirit, and the Spirit against the flesh; for these are in opposition to one another, so that you may not do the things that you please. But if you are led by the Spirit, you are not under the Law. Now the deeds of the flesh are evident, which are: immorality, impurity, sensuality, idolatry, sorcery, enmities, strife, jealousy, outbursts of anger, disputes, dissensions, factions, envying, drunkenness, carousing, and things like these, of which I forewarn you, just as I have forewarned you, that those who practice such things will not inherit the kingdom of God. But the fruit of the Spirit is love, joy, peace, patience, kindness, goodness, faithfulness, gentleness, self-control; against such things there is no law. Now those who belong to Christ Jesus have crucified the flesh with its passions and desires. If we live by the Spirit, let us also walk by the Spirit. Let us not become boastful, challenging one another, envying one another.

Paul describes the flesh and the Spirit as being at odds. He outlines the traits of the flesh such as immorality, idolatry, strife, etc. He also outlines the fruit of the Spirit. Inherently the flesh is at odds with the Spirit. God's given commands are meant to move us by the power of the Holy Spirit in us toward obedience. Augustine in his *Confessions* stated, "Give what thou commandest, and command what thou wilt."[8] The idea is God's commands move God's people to seek his grace and power to obey them, because his grace has opened their eyes to the beauty and glory of Jesus. Evidence of our conversion is often seen in our inward struggle with our own flesh. We hate sin and though we fall into it easily we hate the sin we fall into and desire Jesus. We have a steadfast faith for, like the disciples in John 6:68, we look up to our Lord Jesus in our struggle, crying out, "To whom shall we go, you alone have the words of eternal life." In the midst of the struggle there are times we will feel like we should be further, and in those moments, we fix our eyes on the *finished work* of Jesus and *his future promises*. In the present, we ask God to give us what he commands and to command what he will. Only a creature with a new nature at odds with the old will even have those types of desires and conflicts within him. A Christian is a new creature in Christ per 2 Corinthians 5:17. A converted person will have new desires and will increasingly have a different life. This is because God's Spirit has given them a love for Jesus and they want to walk closely with Jesus and persevere to the end, even as they stumble forward.

I heard a testimony concerning a man who, for the majority of his life, rejected Jesus and had nothing to do with the faith. His wife faithfully loved her husband and loved Jesus. She kept praying for her husband, beseeching God in prayer for him to come to know Jesus. This woman's church called a new pastor who took it upon himself to build a friendship with this woman's husband. Overtime the preacher shared the gospel of Jesus and this man in his seventies was born again. Everything changed. He used to sit and blare the TV when family was over. Now in its place was an open Bible and a man attentive to his family. He used to keep everyone at a distance, after he came to know Jesus he desired to invest in those around him, namely his great grandchildren. He was at service every Sunday and attentive to the Word of God. Yet in all this, he still struggled with sin as we all do. Being a new creation was seen in the trajectory of his desires and life. Yet the presence of sin remained. This man is someone all genuine Christians can

---

8. Quoted in Douglas, "Pelaguis," 546.

identify with to one degree or another. We who know Christ look back at our old selves and barely recognize the person. What we used to love we do not anymore. Hobbies that were so important have lost their taste. Yet even now we are aware of, and struggle with, our sinful flesh and new idols that creep into our hearts. Though much has changed, much still needs to change. We are a people who, in the midst of the command to be holy as God is holy, cling to the reality of vv. 18–21 as our fuel. Verses 18–21 are a reminder of who we were and are now.

## Never Forget!

Never forget! I remember where I was during 9/11. I was a senior in high school when the terrorists flew planes into the Twin Towers. As we watched on TV the horror and evil that was unfolding right before us, the course of our nation's life was altered. After that point, every year at 9/11, there are posts that start out, "Never Forget!" The idea is that we never forget those moments and how we felt on that day. That we never forget what our nation went through which brought us to a time of coming together. We as Christians must never forget, in our present daily struggles and situations, what God has done for us! Peter calls these believers to remember what has happened to them for all time that altered the course of their lives. He states:

> If you address as Father the One who impartially judges according to each one's work, conduct yourselves in fear during the time of your stay *on earth*; knowing that you were not redeemed with perishable things like silver or gold from your futile way of life inherited from your forefathers, but with precious blood, as of a lamb unblemished and spotless, *the blood* of Christ. For He was foreknown before the foundation of the world, but has appeared in these last times for the sake of you who through Him are believers in God, who raised Him from the dead and gave Him glory, so that your faith and hope are in God. (1 Pet 1:17–21)

Peter, once again, begins with the character of God, focusing on his justice in the verbiage of v. 17, and then reminds these believers that they were redeemed, in v. 18, not from their sinful ways that they had inherited by silver or gold, but, in vv. 19–21, they were redeemed by the blood of the unblemished and spotless (sinless) Lamb of God, the Lord Jesus. Jesus who was loved by the father before time was made manifest, God the eternal Son added human flesh by being born in a small town to a peasant woman in Palestine as the world saw it. Peter reminds these believers that they are believers in God. Formerly they were Gentiles ignorant of God's commands, now they are believers in God through Jesus whom God rose from the dead and brought him to the glory he shared with the Father before time. All this, per Peter, results in these believers' faith and hope being in God. They are redeemed. Their lives have been forever altered and they need to remember what altered their lives. It was their redemption in Jesus.

Since I have been redeemed. Since I have been redeemed. I will glory in his name. These are lyrics in the hymn "Since I Have Been Redeemed." The idea is the same one Peter wants these Christians to sing out and rejoice in. The Greek word Peter uses for "redeem" goes back to the institution of slavery in Rome where a price would be provided to procure a servant's freedom.[9] Peter reminds these Christians they were once slaves to sin and under the wrath of God. They were slaves to the "futile" lifestyle of their ancestors. Yet they had been redeemed. The purchase price was not silver or gold, materially the most precious items one could possess. The price was infinitely more valuable than that. It was the blood of Jesus Christ shed on a tree at Calvary. Peter's intention here is clear. Holiness, a disciplined and sober mind, and a faith fixed on the promises of God to be fulfilled at the return of the King of kings, all flow out of a life that has been redeemed by the work of Jesus. Jesus died on the cross to reconcile us to God (justification), to make us continuously more like him in holiness (sanctification), with the end being a perfected people in a perfect place (glorification). As God's redeemed we remember the cross,

9. Barker, "1 Peter," 1045.

we follow our Leader, the sinless Lamb of God, in the present and with his coming glory in mind we wage war daily on our sin. May we not forget this as our daily battle cry!

## Discussion Questions

1. What is the significance of the word "therefore" in this passage of Scripture?

2. What are the five exhortations from Peter concerning living out the faith in the present?

3. What does God is holy mean?

4. What are we never to forget as we struggle in the present?

# 5

## A Steadfast Faith Loves the Church and Proclaims the Gospel

### 1 Peter 1:22–25

*22 Since you have in obedience to the truth purified your souls for a sincere love of the brethren, fervently love one another from the heart,*

*23 for you have been born again not of seed which is perishable but imperishable, that is, through the living and enduring word of God.*

*24 For,*
*"All flesh is like grass,*
*And all its glory like the flower of grass.*
*The grass withers,*
*And the flower falls off,*
*25 But the word of the Lord endures forever."*
*And this is the word which was preached to you.*

IT WAS NIGHT AND a famous rabbi sought the company of a younger, itinerant teacher whose fame was spreading due to his powerful teaching and profound miracles. The older rabbi, possibly moved by an unsettled question about his eternal fate and possibly a desire to talk with a man who must have been from God as each miracle showed, sought the meeting. This older man was named Nicodemus and he was known as The Teacher of Israel. The itinerant teacher was Jesus. As they met in a house, Jesus bypassed the formalities in response to Nicodemus's compliment of being a great teacher and told Nicodemus, "You must be born again to enter the kingdom of God." In that moment Nicodemus's whole worldview busted. He was a Pharisee of Pharisees. His whole life he had kept the law and the tradition of the elders. He thought, in line with the common teaching of the day, that if he was faithful enough and obedient enough his merit would procure God's grace and gain him entrance into the kingdom of God. Jesus told him otherwise. In frustration he cried out, "How can a man be born when he is old? He cannot enter a second time into his mother's womb and be born, can he?" (John 3:4). Jesus responded:

> Truly, truly, I say to you, unless one is born of water and the Spirit he cannot enter into the kingdom of God. That which is born of the flesh is flesh, and that which is born of the Spirit is spirit. Do not be amazed that I said to you, "You must be born again." The wind blows where it wishes and you hear the sound of it, but do not know where it comes from and where it is going; so is everyone who is born of the Spirit. (John 3:5–8)

Nicodemus, exasperated, asked, "How can these things be?" (John 3:9). Jesus responded, "Are you the teacher of Israel and do not understand these things?" (John 3:10). Jesus expected Nicodemus to be familiar with texts in the Old Testament that put forth this truth, such as Ezekiel 36:26–27. Jesus then moved to eventually tell Nicodemus the evidence of being born again, in vv. 14–15: "As Moses lifted up the serpent in the wilderness, even so must the Son of Man be lifted up; so that whoever believes will in Him have eternal life" (John 3:14–15). Jesus conveyed that to be right with God and enter the kingdom of God, you have to be born again, which is evident in a person because they look to the cross of Christ for eternal life. Peter uses this language to convey to those in Asia Minor who were looking to the cross of Christ for life, those who had been born again, that being born again from the gospel should produce a love for all others who are fellow believers in the gospel. We also see in this text the means by which God spreads his church across the world.

## Saved to Love the Church

"I love Jesus, I just do not like the church." "Jesus is greater than religion." These concepts are being put forward and rallied today in our culture. While it is not a negative thing to focus on a personal relationship with Jesus, that personal relationship has ramifications for what we do in life as we saw in the last chapter. It also has great and eternal ramifications for how we connect with and view the church, particularly the sacraments and the local gathering of God's people on a weekly basis around the Word. Jesus does not give us the option to love him and forsake his church. The author of Hebrews bluntly tells those he is writing to, "Let us hold fast the confession of our hope without wavering, for He who promised is faithful; and let us consider how to stimulate one another to love and good deeds, *not forsaking our own assembling together*, as is the habit of some, but encouraging *one another*; and all the more as you see the day drawing near" (Heb 10:23–25). In 1 John 4:18–20 the Apostle John goes as far as to say, "We love, because He first loved us. If someone says, '*I love God*,' and hates his brother, he is a liar; for the one who does not love his brother whom he has seen, cannot love God whom he has not seen. And this commandment we have from Him, that the one who loves God should love his brother also" (1 John 4:19–21, emphasis mine). Being first loved by God, which Peter calls born again in v. 23, produces a love for the church. When you love others then you want to be around them.

By God's grace he has not only saved me but given me a wife who is compassionate, kind, and sacrificial in all she does. She loves Jesus and increasingly longs to know him from his Word rightly divided. I love my wife. I love being around my wife. She is my best friend. How weird would it be to say I love her and yet never spend any time with her? Imagine if the time I dedicated to her mimicked many professing Christians' commitment to the local church. I would only see her a couple times a year and would be mad at her if, during those visits, she didn't meet all my needs. To say I love her but only visit her twice a year on special days would convey something about my true feelings. Our marriage would not last because my profession to love her would be empty and shown to be untrue by my actions. Jesus is so connected to his church that if you distance yourself from the church he sees you as distancing yourself from him. Think about what Jesus said to Saul of Tarsus on the road to Damascus in Acts 9:4, "Saul, Saul, why are you persecuting Me?" (Acts 9:4). Saul was persecuting the church. Jesus was ascended and glorified. However, Jesus saw Saul's persecuting against the church as persecution against him. That is how connected Jesus is to his people. To say we love Jesus but do not like the church is foreign to Christianity in any age. Jesus sees such statements as a denial of our love for him. In essence he says to those who profess to belong to him, "Why do you forsake Me?" Those of us who, as Peter said in 1 Peter 1:22, "have in obedience to the truth purified your souls" are to "fervently love one another from the heart." The principle is clear. If you truly have been born again (1 Pet 1:23) to obedience of the truth we will fervently love the brethren (the church). This means we will desire to spend time with believers in the local church. We will want to gather each week around the Word and gather around the sacraments (baptism and the Lord's Supper). We will want to meet in small groups and serve one another. We will want to do to other believers spiritual good and be accountable to grow with other believers. We will desire to spend time with our local faith family growing in the Word together. We will meet needs of faith family members that we are aware of and can meet. If this type of love does not exist then we should not say, "I love Jesus." When we love his church, we love him; and all those born of the Holy Spirit love Jesus and his church increasingly.

# Dividing the Goats and the Sheep

Jesus is teaching his disciples, after having conveyed in Matthew 24 that the temple they were admiring would be leveled. He has conveyed to them what was to take place leading up to AD 70. In Matthew 25:31–46, Jesus outlines what is to come at his second advent, when he will separate the sheep and the goats. The criteria he uses is fascinating. Let us look at that story briefly.

> But when the Son of Man comes in His glory, and all the angels with Him, then He will sit on His glorious throne.
>
> All the nations will be gathered before Him; and He will separate them from one another, as the shepherd separates the sheep from the goats;
>
> and He will put the sheep on His right, and the goats on the left.
>
> Then the King will say to those on His right, "Come, you who are blessed of My Father, inherit the kingdom prepared for you from the foundation of the world.
>
> For I was hungry, and you gave Me something to eat; I was thirsty, and you gave Me something to drink; I was a stranger, and you invited Me in;
>
> naked, and you clothed Me; I was sick, and you visited Me; I was in prison, and you came to Me."
>
> Then the righteous will answer Him, "Lord, when did we see You hungry, and feed You, or thirsty, and give You something to drink?
>
> And when did we see You a stranger, and invite You in, or naked, and clothe You?
>
> When did we see You sick, or in prison, and come to You?"
>
> *The King will answer and say to them, "Truly I say to you, to the extent that you did it to one of these brothers of Mine, even the least of them, you did it to Me."*
>
> Then He will also say to those on His left, "Depart from Me, accursed ones, into the eternal fire which has been prepared for the devil and his angels;
>
> for I was hungry, and you gave Me *nothing* to eat; I was thirsty, and you gave Me nothing to drink;

> I was a stranger, and you did not invite Me in; na-
> ked, and you did not clothe Me; sick, and in prison, and
> you did not visit Me."
>
> Then they themselves also will answer, "Lord, when
> did we see You hungry, or thirsty, or a stranger, or naked,
> or sick, or in prison, and did not take care of You?"
>
> Then He will answer them, "Truly I say to you, to the
> extent that you did not do it to one of the least of these,
> you did not do it to Me."
>
> These will go away into eternal punishment, but
> the righteous into eternal life. (Matt 25:31–46, emphasis
> mine).

As Jesus told this story, he defined those who entered the kingdom
as those who fed him when he was hungry, when he was a stranger,
they invited him in, clothed him, and visited him when he was
sick. Those on the right asked the question in vv. 38–39, "When
did we see you and do this?" Jesus responds, probably looking out
to the church he redeemed on his right with eyes of love, with,
"Truly I say to you, to the extent that you did it to one of these
brothers of Mine, even the least of them, you did it to Me." Jesus
sees acts of love and service done to his church as love for him and
evidence of their being born again by his Holy Spirit. The goats on
the left also call out to Jesus after he told them that they never fed
him, clothed him, invited him in, or visited him in prison in v. 44,
"When did we ever see you?" Jesus responds that "to the extent you
did not do it to one of the least of these [those on his right] you did
not do it to me." Jesus saw the lack of love and care for the church
as evidence that those on the left did not belong to him and did not
love him. He then put those on the left into everlasting fire. The
implications of this text coupled with what 1 Peter 2:22–23 states is
profound. Those who are born again and purified through obedience to Jesus (those who put their faith in Jesus to save them) will
be shown to be genuine in their service toward, and continual love
of, the local church. No love for the church, no love for Jesus. Do
you love the church and serve those in the church? If the answer is
no then can you really claim to love Jesus per his teaching that his
chief apostle puts forth?

## The Church Grows by
## the Word Being Preached

The church is important. That much is clear per Peter and Jesus, our Lord. The church is God's people, loved eternally by God, and purchased by Jesus. Peter outlines how God builds his church in vv. 23–25 as he quotes Isaiah 40:6 and Isaiah 40:8. Peter states, "For you have been born again not of seed which is perishable but imperishable, *that is*, through the living and enduring word of God. For, 'All flesh is like grass, And all its glory like the flower of grass. The grass withers, And the flower falls off, But the word of the Lord endures forever.' *And this is the word which was preached to you*" (1 Pet 1:23–25, emphasis mine). Peter states that these Christians have been born again by the Word of God being preached to them. He reflects on the passages in Isaiah that display the finite nature of man and the unending nature of God's Word, which encases the gospel of Jesus. Mankind will fade like a flower in the wind, but God's Word endures forever. Peter ends chapter 1 by reminding these Christians that the Word he is talking about here is a particular subject. It is the "word which was preached to you," which was the gospel of Jesus per 1 Peter 1:12. The whole Bible centers around the glory of God in Jesus as seen in the gospel. We dove into that in chapter 3. As this gospel is preached, people come out of spiritual darkness and deadness by the power of the Holy Spirit. They come out of darkness into the church. The church grows in number as the gospel is preached, as the Word of God is expounded.

## The Church Is Built on the Word

Jesus told Peter in Matthew 16:17–18, "Blessed are you, Simon Barjona, because flesh and blood did not reveal this to you, but My Father who is in heaven. 'I also say to you that you are Peter, and upon *this rock I will build My church; and the gates of Hades will not overpower it*'" (Matt 16:17–18, emphasis mine). Jesus is the one who builds his church and he does it from his word preached as we saw in 1 Peter 1:25. As the word is preached Jesus will build for himself a people from every tribe, tongue, and nation redeemed by him (Matt 24:14; Rev 7:9–10).

The Bible never describes the church as many today refer to it. I have heard so many people say, "I'm going to church." What they mean by that is that they are going to a building for a service. Going to a certain location, while not a bad thing, is not the point. The Bible depicts the church with the Greek word *ecclesia*, which means "assembly." The word in the New Testament is used in a variety of ways. First, the word is used to describe a local group of people in a community who are redeemed in the Lord Jesus, are baptized in Christ, and who meet weekly in order to grow in knowledge and grace together (Rom 16:5; Col 4:15). The word *ecclesia* also describes Christians from all ages, meaning the redeemed of God bought by Christ from every era and every people group (Eph 5:23, 25, 27, 29; Heb 12:23). Next, the word *ecclesia* is used to describe Christians made up of many churches in a particular city or region in the New Testament (Acts 13:1; 1 Cor 1:2; Acts 8:1; Rev 2:1). Lastly, the word *ecclesia* is employed to describe the redeemed living in this age alone (1 Cor 15:9; Gal 1:13; Matt 16:18). Nevertheless, the basic the fundamental definition of the church is the gathered, redeemed of Jesus around his gospel and grace for his glory.

What is amazing is *the Lord Jesus accomplishes his mission of building his church through his church.* Peter conveys this later in this epistle when he states, "But you are a chosen race, a royal priesthood, a holy nation, a people for *God's* own possession, so that *you may proclaim the excellencies of Him who has called you out of darkness into His marvelous light*" (1 Pet 2:9, emphasis mine). We as his people, are the covenant people of God who are to inherit all the promises, which is why Peter used the language he did in v. 9 of ch. 2, with the mission of proclaiming God's excellencies in all the world. The church is the means by which God proclaims his truth to all nations and the church is to cover all nations and people groups as the temple of God on earth (1 Pet 2:1–9).

## What Does That Mean for Me?

Jesus loves his church and is building his church with people from every people group. That means that as we go through life, wherever we find ourselves per God's sovereignty, we share the gospel knowing that God's people will come forth. We seek to intentionally pour our lives out for the spread of the gospel. We look to utilize our gifts and resources to take the gospel to the unreached and unengaged (those with no access to the gospel). We share the works of God culminating in Christ (the excellencies of him who called you out of darkness into his marvelous light), knowing Jesus will have his reward. People will be saved as the gospel is preached. God will draw his people out of the world! The Great Commission becomes a daily reality wherever we find ourselves (Matt 28:19–20). Thank about our commission which our Lord Jesus gave to the apostles (the foundation of the church) before his ascension.

> And Jesus came up and spoke to them, saying, *"All authority has been given to Me in heaven and on earth.*
>
> Go therefore and make disciples of all the nations, baptizing them in the name of the Father and the Son and the Holy Spirit,
>
> teaching them to observe all that I commanded you; and lo, *I am with you always, even to the end of the age."* (Matt 28:18–20, emphasis mine)

Jesus began the commission by reminding his followers that all authority is his. He ends the commission by reminding his followers he is with them to the end of the age. Between those two statements is the church's marching orders. However, it is the fact of Jesus' authority over all nations and the reality that *he is always with us* that compels us to proclaim him to the world. What do we, as God's people, need to fear? We serve the all-powerful, all-knowing, fully-everywhere-at-all-times King who promises to never leave us for a moment in time. With great confidence, we share the gospel as we go through life knowing the work of salvation is God's work through his people. We know that we cannot bring anyone to salvation in our human persuasiveness but the work to bring a people to "a steadfast faith" is the work of God and it will not fail. Jesus rules over all. The Holy Spirit alone regenerates hearts of stone (spiritually dead people). Our family, our neighbors, our communities, our nation, and all nations need to hear this news, the gospel of God. The church is the buttress of truth and has the keys of the kingdom. We go to our neighbors and the nations to open the door for them, but only the Spirit of God causes them to walk through. Only the Spirit of God brings forth a steadfast faith in the object of the biblical Jesus. A steadfast faith in Jesus is one that looks to him to cover all our sins, to remake us daily in his image and propel us to love the church and proclaim his message, as he continually raises our gaze to his coming glory! Is the steadfast faith of Peter your brand of faith? Remember there is only one faith, once and for all, delivered to the saints (Jude 1:3).

## Discussion Questions

1. What does it mean to be born again?
2. Can we truly love Jesus but not love the church?
3. How does Jesus relate loving him to loving the church?
4. How does God build his church and what part are we to play in that process?

# Bibliography

Barker, Kenneth L., ed. *The Expositor's Bible Commentary: New Testament.* Abridged ed. Grand Rapids: Zondervan, 1994.

Barry, John D., et al., eds. *The Lexham Bible Dictionary.* Bellingham, WA: Lexham, 2016.

Brand, Chad, et al., eds. *Holman Illustrated Bible Dictionary.* Nashville: Holman, 2003.

Calvin, John. *Institutes of Christian Religion.* Bk. 1, ch. 11, sec. 8. Translated by Henry Beveridge. Peabody: Hendrickson, 2008.

Douglas, James Dixon. "Pelagius." In *Who's Who in Christian History*, edited by J. D. Douglas and P. W. Comfort, 546. Wheaton, IL: Tyndale, 1992.

Galli, Mark, and Ted Olsen. *131 Christians Everyone Should Know.* Nashville: Broadman & Holman, 2000.

Geisler, Norman L. "A Note of the Percent of Accuracy of the New Testament Text." https://normangeisler.com/a-note-on-the-percent-of-accuracy-of-the-new-testament-text/.

Geisler, Norman L., and William E. Nix. *A General Introduction to the Bible.* Rev. ed. Chicago: Moody, 1986.

Grudem, Wayne. *Systematic Theology.* Grand Rapids: Zondervan, 1994.

Haykin, Michael A. G., and C. Jeffrey Robinson Sr. *To the Ends of the Earth: Calvin's Missional Vision and Legacy.* Wheaton, IL: Crossway, 2014.

Howard, Dave M. "Elliot, Philip James." In *Who's Who in Christian History*, James Dixon D. and Philip W. Comfort, 230. Wheaton, IL: Tyndale, 1992.

Kittel, Gerhard, et al., eds. *Theological Dictionary of the New Testament.* Grand Rapids: Eerdmans, 1985.

Lewis, C. S. *Mere Christianity.* New York: HarperOne, 2001.

———. *Reflections on the Psalms.* New York: Harcourt, Brace, Jovanovich, 1964.

Louw, Johannes P., and Eugene A. Nida. *Greek-English Lexicon of the New Testament: Based on Semantic Domains.* Vol. 1. Electronic ed. of 2nd ed. New York: United Bible Societies, 1996.

Newport, Frank. "2017 Update on Americans and Religion." Gallup. December 22, 2017. https://news.gallup.com/poll/224642/2017-update-americans-religion.aspx.

## Bibliography

Patterson, Ben, and David L. Goetz. *Deepening Your Conversation with God.* Vol. 7. Minneapolis: Bethany House, 1999.

Raymer, Roger M. "1 Peter." In *The Bible Knowledge Commentary: An Exposition of the Scriptures,* edited by John F. Walvoord and Roy B. Zuck, 2:837–58. Wheaton, IL: Victor, 1985.

Schreiner, Thomas R. *1, 2 Peter, Jude.* New American Commentary 37. Nashville: Broadman & Holman, 2003.

Sproul, R. C., and Stephen J. Nichols. *The Legacy of Luther.* Sanford, FL: Reformation Trust, 2016.

Swanson, James. *Dictionary of Biblical Languages with Semantic Domains: Greek (New Testament).* Electronic ed. Oak Harbor: Logos, 1997.

Tan, Paul Lee. *Encyclopedia of 7,700 Illustrations: Signs of the Times.* Garland, TX: Bible Communications, 1996.

www.ingramcontent.com/pod-product-compliance
Lightning Source LLC
Chambersburg PA
CBHW070515090426
42735CB00012B/2793